Debt Free
The Morals of Money Management
How to live within your means and be happy

W. J. SCOTT

Illustrations by
ANDREW SCOTT

© All rights reserved Felix Publishing 2016

© **All rights reserved Felix Publishing 2016**

**2016 -ebook update (English)
ISBN: 978-0-99457550-2-4**

2015 e-book release (English):
ISBN: 978-0-9944452-2-3
2015 paperback release (English):
ISBN: 978-0-9944452-3-0
2015 e-book release (Spanish)
ISBN:978-0-9944452-6-1
2015 paperback release (Spanish):
ISBN:978-0-9944452-7-8

First released and printed in 2015 by Rico Bruesch Publishing

Author: W. J. Scott

Illustrations: Andrew Scott

Registration:
Thorpe-Bowker
Level 1, 607 St Kilda Road
Melbourne, VIC 3000, Australia
Tel: +61 3 8517 8342
e-mail: bowkerlink@thorpe.com.au

No part of this publication may be reproduced, stored in a retrieval system, or transmitted in any form or by any means, electronic, mechanical, photocopying, recording or otherwise, without the prior written permission of the author or publisher.

This book is written for all those who have ever asked me" how I can live comfortably with sufficient money for all of my needs, most of my wants, and be debt free?", and to all of the students and bankers who have asked for this book to be written. I hope it will be simple enough to understand without needing a prior knowledge of finances, but detailed enough to get you out of debt and back in control without having to pay others enormous amounts of money to do it for you.

I dedicate this to my husband Dr. Peter Scott who encouraged me to write this book, and our two sons Matthew and Andrew.

ACKNOWLEDGEMENTS

A special acknowledgement goes to my son, Andrew Scott, for creating all the lovely illustrations in this book.

Acknowledgement goes to Dr. Rico Brüesch, for his input in the following chapters for me: Debt Collectors; Bankruptcy & Other Debt Options; Divorces; E.P.A's & G.P.A.'s; A.H.D.'s; and Insurance.

A minimum of 10% of the sales of this book will go towards the following charities:

Médicins Sans Frontières, World Vision, Cancer Council and Alzheimers Australia.

DISCLAIMER

THIS IS A MUST READ SECTION

Now for the disclaimers:

This information is of a general nature and not intended to replace qualified financial and legal advice based on your specific circumstances. You are advised to seek appropriate financial advice before investing, taking out any loan, or buying that new shiny thing that you just can't live without. Make sure you know how the advisor is paid, and if higher commissions are paid for specific investments. The advice may not always be in your best interests, but in his or hers.

The information in this book is from my own ideas formulated from painful financial experiences with shonky estate agents, dubious financial advisers and formal training and qualifications as a financial adviser, teacher, and counsellor. I hope you will learn from my mistakes without making them yourselves, as well as copying what I did correctly if it is appropriate to your circumstances.

CONTENTS

Copyright	i
Dedication	ii
Acknowledgements	iii
Disclaimer	iv
Foreword	ix
Summary	xi
Ch 1 Introduction	1
Ch 2 SevenVirtues	4
2.1 Faith	
2.2 Hope.	
2.3 Charity.	
2.4 Justice	
2.5 Prudence	
2.6 Temperance	
2.7Courage/Fortitude	
Ch 3 Seven Vices	46
3.1 Lust	
3.2 Gluttony	
3.3 Greed	
3.4 Sloth	
3.5 Wrath	

3.6 Envy
3.7 Pride

Ch 4 Education 69

Ch 5 Banking 73

Ch 6 Buying & Owning a House 82

Ch 7 Debt Collectors 93

Ch 8 Bankruptcy & Other Debt Options 98

Ch 9 Investing 107
9.1 Rental property
9.2 Shares
9.3 Superannuation

Ch 10 Buying Things 116

Ch 11 Mobile Phones 118

Ch 12 Weddings 124

Ch 13 Divorces 129

Ch 14 Retirement 134

Ch 15 Wills 139

Ch 16 E.P.A. & G.P.A 146

Ch 17 A.H.D	**152**
Ch 18 Insurance	**155**
Ch 19 Toys	**170**
Ch 20 Children	**173**
Ch 21 The Budget	**180**
Ch 22 Epilogue	**183**
Ch 23 Useful Links	**185**
About the author	**203**
Availability	**204**

FOREWORD

How this book is set up... This is the cheat sheet...

Each chapter will have a theme and topic with examples, good (what to do) and bad (what not to do). The first paragraph will be an outline, so you know what to expect. Each section will then be explained in detail with illustrations, examples and the consequences of following or not following the suggestions. This book is designed for almost anyone, whether you're a high school student who just got their first part-time job, or are a mature person who has two or three maxed out credit cards. For most of us it is a chance to reevaluate what you are doing right and what small changes you could make to improve your life.

The purpose of this book is to allow you to get in control of your finances, and have the confidence and freedom of knowing a debt collector won't be knocking on your door. You will be able to be generous with others, kind to yourself, and live on whatever funds you have in comfort and peace. If you own your own home by 40, have shares and an investment property or two, enjoy regular holidays and give generously to charity whilst helping your family, that's a bonus, but not guaranteed. Being debt free is a reality that you can choose for yourself and your family.

All suggestions in this book are comprised of general advice for people without formal qualifications in tax law, accountancy, stockbroking, real estate investment or experience in setting up and operating hedge funds. This book is not intended for those with an accounting and investment team, or who have their own personal management department in their own multinational company. This book is also not designed for the "mature or wholesale investors." (You want to stay away from anything that states it is only for "mature or wholesale investors," which is very, very, very high risk, where you could lose everything.) At the end of each chapter you will find a short summary containing a list of the main points within that chapter.

SUMMARY

The choices are yours. You can choose to follow the concepts in this book and live debt free. How much you benefit from it will depend on YOU, your circumstances and the choices you make. How you use this book depends on whether you are revising, scanning, reading or putting it into practice. Each method works, but using a combination of all these methods seems to work the best.

Topic, overview, explanation, summary, dot points.

- Your choices,
- Your lifestyle.

Chapter 1
INTRODUCTION

All belief systems, formal and informal, have tenets by which to live in harmony with others, even those who choose not to follow a religion have a philosophy for living. The philosophy that I have chosen is the seven virtues and vices from the Bible as the wisdom is timeless, and the concepts are similar in most belief systems. Many people are familiar with the wisdom of Solomon, in the Book of Proverbs in the Old Testament, warning of the seven deadly sins. These sins are: lust; gluttony; greed; sloth; wrath; envy; and pride. These seven deadly sins are contrasted with the seven virtues of faith, which include: faith; hope; charity; justice; prudence; temperance; and fortitude.

When practiced, the seven deadly vices can destroy any hope of financial independence. Whereas, practicing the seven virtues of faith will guide you towards a financially sound and fulfilled life. (Notice that I did not say fabulously wealthy and driving a Ferrari... It may happen, but you would need to start at an early age.) Some of the world's richest men and women operate on a similar system to what I'm describing in this book. Some of them are the greatest philanthropists, Bill Gates

CHAPTER 1

and Warren Buffett are, whilst others are not. There are no guarantees in your life, but the choices you make determine your luck, whether good or bad.

Before you seek advice from someone claiming to be a professional trying to encourage you to invest in a sure thing: REMEMBER: THE GREATER THE PROMISED RETURN, THE GREATER THE RISK! You could make a lot of money, or more likely, accumulate a lot more debt.

Whatever money you can't afford to lose, do not bet on the stock market, invest in hedge funds, put into poker machines, bet on horses, invest in tree farms, or place into schemes for mature investors or wholesale investors promising an attractive 10% to 100% return. I will mention more on this in the section on Greed.

A sure thing does not exist!

Summary:

Investments mean risk, so if you cannot afford to lose it, DO NOT INVEST IT!

Being virtuous and showing faith, hope, charity, justice, prudence, temperance, and fortitude (courage) should improve your life and your finances. However, following the sins of lust, gluttony, greed, sloth, wrath, envy, and pride are more likely to leave you empty, poor, and friendless.

CHAPTER 1

- Who you are matters.

- What you do matters.

- If you cannot afford to lose it, do not risk it.

- A sure thing does not exist.

Chapter 2

THE SEVEN VIRTUES

FAITH

HOPE

CHARITY

JUSTICE

PRUDENCE

TEMPERANCE

COURAGE / FORTITUDE

Faith

Faith determines what is important to you and what you value. Faith in a Supreme Being, such as God, or in a formal religion means that you will be guided by the tenets of that religion. For example, in a perfect world, a Christian, a Moslem, a Jew or a Hindu would never kill, steal or lie. Someone who does not subscribe to a formal religion, but believes in Karma and protecting the environment, would not kill steal or lie either for exactly the same reasons. The Golden Rule states: "Do unto others as you would have them do unto you." Your faith is your focus, and how you interact with others. What you believe in determines who you are.

As I am most familiar with the Christian Faith, I will write about the Christian points of view throughout this section. Those with a different ethos should substitute their own beliefs where appropriate.

From the Christian point of view you are required to look after the money you have and not waste it. You are also instructed to help the poor and give to the work of the church. Therefore you shouldn't spend your money wildly without regard to how much you have, so that you can make sure that you are able to help others. I will refrain from quoting from the Bible, to avoid offending those with other beliefs. However, should you wish to google any of the main ideas in this section you will be able to locate the relevant verses, as I will be specific enough to allow you to find them, but still remain general enough to keep the focus on the financial issues.

If you believe it is your duty to help the poor, refugees, widows, orphans and those who are sick, you can't expect to fulfil that duty if you spend all your money before you receive your pay. Christians, Jews, and Moslems are all required to be good stewards of their money, which means they should use, share, and invest their money wisely. It does not mean you should give up everything and expect others to look after your family. It also does not mean that you should spend everything on drinking, gambling, and generally wasting your money. The middle path of social, moral and family responsibility is the way to go.

No mainstream religion promotes alcohol until oblivion takes over. Therefore, if you must drink, do it in moderation without any binge drinking. Not consuming any alcohol at all will free up a lot of cash for clearing debts, saving for a house, or buying a car. How can you really enjoy life if you are so drugged that you are incapable of rational thought and have to steal or resort to prostitution to support those habits?

Do not start taking recreational drugs. You do not know if you are part of the majority of those who will suffer from serious side effects. Most recreational drugs require just one use and within 3 seconds you become a lifelong addict. Your family suffers just as much, if not more than you. The money required to maintain your addiction is huge. The physical, emotional and social costs are just too high. For example, if you are convicted there are many jobs closed to you forever. Such jobs include: most government positions; mortgage brokers; bank manager; taxi driver; security officer; real estate agent; accountant; lawyer; some construction professions, and teachers... The list is almost endless... Also, you will no longer be able to travel to countries such as the USA, Singapore, or to the Middle East. You would have to suffer a lifetime of wearing the consequences of having a record of a previous jail sentence. Quitting is so hard, it's easier not to start in the first place.

Smoking is also another addictive drug. It affects you on three levels, physical, chemical and psychological. Do not start, or if you have... STOP! In Australia you can contact Quitline on 13 78 48, or visit their website www.quitnow.gov.au. The money you save by not smoking one pack of cigarettes a day could save you enough cash within two years to buy a new car. Another benefit is your health and body odour will improve out of sight!

The purpose is of book is to help you help yourself. You will know you have achieved this when your children say: "Off spending our inheritance again?" or "Going on ski holidays again? Well done, keep it up." You note that they didn't say, "How did you get the money for that?" or "How will you be able to pay the mortgage?"

How to do it?

- Keep aside 10% for helping others.

- If you do not need it, do not buy it.

- Do not spend what you do not have.

- Save 10% from every pay for emergencies do not touch it unless you find yourself out of a job, or for hospital fees, etc.

- Save 10% for a house deposit.

FAITH

- Make sure your house repayments, or rent, do not exceed 30% of your base wage.

- Put aside 30% of your base wage before you get your take home pay. You will not miss it if you don't have access to it in the first place. Live simply with fresh fruit and vegetables and meats which are in season, they are a cheaper and a healthier alternative. Then, do all your own cooking, pack your own lunch, and make your tea or coffee at work. By doing this you cut your food expenses in half. A person who purchases a Starbucks coffee on their way to work ($5.25) and eats take away food for lunch each day ($12.50) wastes $4,260 a year on unnecessary takeaway food, assuming they cook their own dinner at home after work, otherwise it would be even more. Cereal in a bowl with milk is quicker and better for you than cartons of instant breakfast or takeaway muffins and a drink. The amount that you save by not buying breakfast or your morning coffee one day a week alone could support a child with World Vision or pay half of an eye surgery through the Fred Hollows Foundation or keep a doctor working with Médecins san Frontiers. Small changes have a big payoff.

The best part is that you and your family will feel good about being able to give to those in need of sight, food and education, or provide doctors in places where there are none. This benefits your own health too! Your physical and emotional health will improve because you used fresh food at home and the savings are productive. You also save by not needing those extra sick days off work, and visits to your doctor as often. I love win, win, win, situations!

Faith:

- **Look after yourself.**

- **Look after others in need'**

- **Live within your means.**

- **Love one another.**

HOPE

<u>Hope</u>

Right now, if you are reading this you are probably not a millionaire, but if you follow this book you might even become one. No guarantees, but who knows? If you are already a millionaire, by now you would have given at least $100,000 to help others. Imagine that! Making sure that you know exactly what you have, and that your money is working for you, is the crux of this.

Many people who are in debt, give up hope and then spend what they have on things to try to make themselves feel better. Such people continuously buy shiny things such as the latest i-thing, gizmo, gadget or computer game, etc. Others try to get drunk to drown their sorrows, try to win it back on the pokies, buy a new dress or shoes on the credit card, or eat themselves to obesity. None of these things work, instead they just make the situation worse.

Hope can be restored by your working to get back in control of your finances. Consolidating debts only works if you pay them off faster instead of creating more.

I am going to use the 'B word' here, **BUDGET!**

With a positive attitude of hope you can take a realistic approach to your finances, by knowing how much money comes in, goes out, and where.

For one whole week keep a list of everything that comes in and goes out. Note down and keep receipts for all those tap-and-go purchases. Have a small notebook where you write down every cent. Doing this for just one week will make you very aware of how frequently you spend, how much you spend, and how much you have to show for it at the end of the week. The most surprising thing is you realise how much comes in.

Once you have done this, look at your bank accounts, credit cards, charge cards and store cards. How much are you paying to operate them? Add up all the annual fees, transaction charges, and the interest rates you are paying. If you have savings accounts, make sure you are not paying account keeping fees for them. Make sure you are getting the best interest rates and the best access.

HOPE

You can go online to websites such as www.infochoice.com.au/banking to compare various accounts. Alternatively, many banks will sit down with you and show you how you can avoid fees and charges while maximising your interest. They do this in the hope that you will remain their loyal customer. You probably will be, if they show integrity and really care for you. Keep them on your side, they can help.

Be positive about the amount of money you bring in. It does not matter how large or how small that amount is. What really matters is how you live with the amount you have.

Plan to succeed! If you are in financial distress, it took you time and energy to get into distress, therefore you can expect that it will take just as much time and energy to reverse that.

Work out what you have. Work out what you **NEED,** not want. Set aside money for what you need, and use the rest for repaying debts sooner and for saving. Only when you have repaid all that you owe will you be free to indulge yourself. If you use debt (i.e. someone else's money) to indulge yourself and can't pay the debt back, that would be just like stealing. (Bankruptcy laws were brought in to protect those unfortunate people who became unable to pay their debts because of unforeseen catastrophic circumstances, such as floods, or bushfires which destroyed all they had, so they would not have to be an eternal slave to their creditors. It was never intended to get people out of trouble because of their own stupidity. Many countries do not have bankruptcy laws. When you are unable to pay your debts those countries treat it the same as stealing.)

Do not give up hope.

Negotiate with those to whom you owe money.

When it comes to debts, pay off as much as you can, as quickly as you can. Interest is crippling. (Credit card providers in Australia now have to display on each credit card statement how much interest you will pay on your balance if you only repay the minimum amount. At 24.95% p.a. interest your credit card debt would double in 2 years and 9 months, at 19.99% p.a. it will double in 3 years and 5 months, and at 9.99% p.a. it will double in 6 years and 11 months.)

If you cannot pay a medical bill ask the doctor for time to pay off the balance. Most will happily cooperate. Do not be tempted to get a payday loan just to save embarrassment. Ask, and you will be surprised how many people will help. Do not wait until the bill is overdue to negotiate, then it will be too late to get favourable terms. The same is true for electricity and gas providers, and telecommunication companies.

NEVER GET A PAYDAY LOAN

NEVER GET A PAYDAY LOAN

NEVER GET A PAYDAY LOAN

HOPE

Interest on payday loans currently charge around 4% compounding interest each month (that's 160% per year!). Plus an additional 20% of the initial loan amount. Therefore, if you borrow $100 to purchase a new dress for a party it will cost you at least $280 within the first year. This is assuming that you pay all repayments on time and that there are no late fees, or penalty interest. I used the most up-to-date figures from six of the most popular payday lenders. You can check them out yourself using the following website:

www.finder.com.au/payday-loans/compare

When it comes to payday loans, be very scared over the startup fees, usually 20%, which is in addition to their 4% compounding interest per month.

Someone else could be wearing the same dress, or you stain it with wine and never wear it again. Was it really worth it?

Instead you could enjoy a picnic in a park, go bushwalking, or pack a little two man tent to go camping. Live with joy! These things cost very little. Do not bemoan what you have not got, but instead you should celebrate what you have. There are many people in the world who have nothing to wear, new or otherwise. They do not have enough to eat and probably nowhere safe to live. If you could afford this book, then you are more fortunate than the majority of the world's population.

Live with hope. Things will improve, but only if you cut waste, stick to a budget and save.

Hope:

- **What do you have.**

- **What do you need.**

- **Budget, and stick to it.**

- **Negotiate terms.**

- **Celebrate all that you have.**

CHARITY

<u>Charity</u>

Charity is also called love. Caring for others as you would like to be cared for yourself. It is not, and should never be a way to belittle others. It is sharing what you have in abundance, which could be your time, expertise, goods or money.

If you are passionate about what you give to others, there are three benefits. Firstly, you feel great being able to help someone. Furthermore, you see how someone else benefits. Finally, our tax laws provide you with generous tax concession to thank you for your philanthropy. It's a win, win, win situation!

If you are passionate about a charity group, such as The Fred Hollows Foundation, a small gift of $25 could help restore someone's sight. How good would that make you feel? For the price of a lunch for one, at an average café or bistro, you can restore freedom and sight to someone you may never meet, and change their life from dependence to freedom. A similar donation to the World Wildlife Fund could save precious habitats for an endangered species. A donation to Lifeline could provide a counsellor to give hope and save the life of someone desperate, or provide emergency accommodation to a mother and her children escaping domestic violence.

The passion that you feel giving to the charity of your choice helps improve your mood and your health. Society as a whole also benefits when charities are assisted through private donations. As a result our government will often match donations made to those charities. Consequently, our government feels that you, the kind donor, should not just benefit from the donation through improved mood and health, they feel that you should benefit financially too!

Currently the tax rules in Australia are set up in such a way that you receive a tax deduction for donations made to any registered charity. What this means is that if you give $100 to a charity and your marginal tax rate on that

CHARITY

$100 is 42%, then you do not have to pay that 42% tax on the amount of money you donated. Effectively in this case you would have received a $42 tax deduction. The overall benefit to the charity could even be as high as double the amount of your donation, if there is a dollar-for-dollar donation matching scheme for that charity. Around June each year, our government targets certain charities that perform overseas health and education work, and for that month only our government co-contributes up to five dollars for every dollar you donate to those charities. Therefore, for every one dollar you donate, that charity receives a total of six dollars. If you have previously given to charities such as the Uniting World Education Fund, they will inform you when the five to one donation matching starts. Our government does this to increase its overseas aid.

According to ATO's website: For you to claim a tax deduction for a gift, it must meet the following five conditions:

- The gift must be made to a deductible gift recipient. We call entities that are entitled to receive tax deductible gifts 'deductible gift recipients' (DGRs).

  - The gift must truly be a gift. A gift is voluntary transfer of money or property where you receive no material benefit or advantage.
  - The gift must be money or property, which includes financial assets such as shares.

- The gift must comply with any relevant gift conditions. For some DGRs, the income tax law adds extra conditions affecting the types of deductible gifts they can receive.
- For gifts of money, it is the amount of the gift but it must be $2 or more.

If that's not enough to make you feel better, and if you are generous with your donations, you could even manage to drop yourself into a lower marginal tax bracket. That would save you even more, which will make you feel really good!

Did you realise that you can also shop in charity stores? By doing so, you can often get unique designer brands for very little money. Many items will still have their original swing tags. On top of that, you will also be giving money to that charity instead of supporting a foreign owned multinational company. It's a win, win, win for everyone!

Charity

- **Donations benefit your mood.**

- **Donations benefit your health.**

- **Donations benefit your tax return.**

- **Donations directly benefit your charity.**

CHARITY

- **Donations also indirectly benefit your charity.**

- **Charity shopping is fun and good value.**

JUSTICE

JUSTICE

Justice requires you to treat others fairly and without prejudice. It also means that you should treat yourself fairly too. Therefore, if you see an injustice done, do what you can to correct it. This does not mean that you are able to control the outcome. You can only control how you behave towards others.

Put simply, "Just because you can, does not mean you should!"

JUSTICE

When you have a payment that is due, it means that you have entered into a contract to buy or borrow something. The person or company, who needs to be paid, has provided you with a service, or loaned you money. Therefore, if you have received their service on time, and at the agreed standard, you should pay their account as soon as you are able. If the loan was right and fair and your repayment is due you should pay as soon as you can. This does not mean that you wait until the day it becomes due to pay it.

Although you could decide to pay the account on the due date and collect the little interest in your account, rather than letting them have the money straight away. Is this really being fair and just? They might be counting on your payment to pay their accounts or staff, or suffering from cash flow problems. Several things could happen to you. You may accidentally spend that money and be unable to pay on the due date. The due date could occur on the weekend or public holiday, so the bank does not transfer the funds on that day. You could be busy and forget, or you could be away. The result would be the same. Your payment will be late.

There are many consequences for late payments, which include:

- late fees
- interest charges
- a bad payment note on your credit rating (this could stop you getting loans and credit cards,

or result in you paying higher interest rates).

Paying early, as soon as you are able, means:

- on-time discounts
- good credit rating
- lower interest rates (less interest to pay on loans)

What if the item you purchased is substandard, or the work agreed is incomplete, and you have tried all forms of negotiation in trying to get the problem rectified? Keep a paperwork trail. Keep a record of phone calls. Keep all email correspondences. Make sure you put this in writing and contact the appropriate ombudsman or builders' licensing authority. Refer to the Australian Consumer Law www.consumerlaw.gov.au. (which lists the rights and remedies for Australian consumer disputes). It tells you how to go about settling disputes. You can find a list of useful websites to contact for your specific dispute at the back of this book.

If an item you purchase is substandard, take it back. You are entitled to a full refund under Australian law, if it is not of a usable condition, fit for the intended purpose, not as described, or if a reasonable person would not have bought it aware of the condition it was in. Ignore the signs that say no refunds on sale items. Such signs are illegal in Australia. You have the absolute right to get a full refund for faulty goods, and you are not obliged to accept store credit or a replacement unless you choose to

JUSTICE

do so. At all times in your negotiations, make sure that you are courteous and respectful. Do not abuse the salesperson, as it is not their fault, and it would not be fair that they should not have to put up with abuse at work. However, you do not have a right to any refund if you simply change your mind. You bought it, so it is yours.

Justice can only happen if everyone's rights are respected. The six moral principles are:

1. "Do unto others as you would have them do unto you" - The Golden Rule

2. "If an action is not right for everyone to take, it is not right for anyone" - Immanuel Kant's Categorical Imperative

3. "If an action cannot be taken repeatedly, it is not right to take at all" - Descartes' rule of change

4. "Take the action that achieves the highest or greater value" - Utilitarian Principle

5. "Take the action that produces the least harm or has the least potential cost" - Risk Aversion Principle

6. "Whatever goods and services have been provided, must be paid for by someone" - No Free Lunch Rule

Justice

- Just because you can, does that mean you should?

- Do you expect others to treat you justly?

- Protect yourself and others. If you see an injustice done, do what you can to correct it!

PRUDENCE

PRUDENCE

Prudence is the key to living within your means. It means being aware of the consequences of your actions, and always choosing the action that allows you to live in harmony with your neighbours, not being wasteful, and saving to meet your own future and present needs.

Obey the law - it is prudent to do so!

PRUDENCE

If you expect to be protected by the law, so no one steals that which you have worked hard for, or do not get attacked when you walk down the street, or run over by a car, then you are also responsible for obeying the law.

When completing your annual tax return, remember, if you did not spend it do not claim it. This saves you getting fined as a result of a tax audit.

Keeping your dogs under control and on a leash in public saves you being a pariah (social outcast.) It saves others from injury as well. It also saves you from receiving a fine or the destruction of a loved pet.

When you drive a car the speed limits are just that, the limit and not the recommended driving speed! It's worth mentioning something that most people do not realise. If the speed limit is 60 km/hr, then you could be fined for driving at 60 km/hr because you are not supposed to be driving at the limit, but you should be driving below the limit. It works the same way as a driver is deemed to be driving drunk when at the blood alcohol limit, because the law states you must drive below the speed limit, or below a certain alcohol level. They may allow for a tolerance of errors in measurement precision, but don't count on it, as seen in a recent news article:

http://www.9news.com.au/National/2015/06/02/10/52/Queensland-man-fined-for-sticking-to-speed-limit)

So don't cry when you get a fine, lose your licence, your car insurance increases, or you get jail time for harming

PRUDENCE

others. The same goes for drunk driving, driving under influence of drugs or medication that can affect your coordination, texting, illegal u-turns at traffic lights, and not wearing a seat belt, etc. The police are not harassing you they are simply doing their job when you choose to break the law.

These are just a few examples but the consequences are similar. Fines cost you money that could have been spent elsewhere. Driving infringements increase your insurance premium and may lead to loss of licence. Jail time reduces your chances of employment, travel and can destroy your family.

Respect others, it is prudent and decent!

If you respect others you will have their wellbeing as well as your own in mind in all of your actions. Generally, the better you treat others, the better you are treated. This means you are more likely to acquire and keep a good job, and are more likely to be happier and healthier as a result.

Only get what you need!

If you buy a whole lot of things that you want, but do not need, you will just end up with huge debts. You do not need the latest computer. Instead, use the library's computers for free. Your phone does not need upgrading if it still works. You do not need pay TV, or Netflix, the programmes are similar to those on free to air. You do not need takeaway lunches, pack your lunch or eat at

PRUDENCE

home. Your children to not need the latest toys, they need your love and attention! Try joining toy swaps and visiting charity shops for toys. You do not need name brand clothing, just wear something clean and neat. You may want this year's latest i-thing, but you do not need them. For the cost of a new iPhone (approximately $1,200), you could pay your council rates or electricity accounts for the year. Remember, you cannot avoid utility bills, but you can surely avoid the advertising and social pressure to show off your new toy.

You need to pay your rent, or mortgage, because you have a contract. If you cannot afford it, downsize. This means you live within your means. If you use electricity or gas you pay for it, so do not waste it. Don't use air-conditioners if a fan will do. Turn off any unused appliances and do not light rooms that no one is in. Only buy the food you can eat before it expires. According to statistics Australian households throw out a massive 30% of the food they have bought. What a waste!

Look after all that you have!

Wash your clothes regularly. Insects love food stains and tend to eat holes in your clothes, if you have a teenage horizontal wardrobe (clothes strewn all over the floor). This could mean that your favourite jeans could become destroyed just because of a simple pizza stain. Maintaining your bike, car and other possessions will ensure they last longer, operate more efficiently, and save you money. Remember, maintenance is considerably cheaper than repairs.

Look after yourself!

Eat well and drink lots of water and exercise (bottled water is an environmental disaster and is usually less fit to drink than tap water in Australia). Walking is free, and you need no equipment. Swimming at the beach is free too. Dancing is great fun, so you do not really need those gym fees. Vigorously cleaning the house is one of the best methods of getting an all over body workout, with the extra benefit of a clean and healthy house. This is not gender specific, so men can do it too! If you use it, or you make the mess, you should clean it. This will reduce your medical bills and distress. You also need to take time out to relax and enjoy yourself, for the same reason.

Prudence

- **Be nice to everyone, save and only get what you need.**

- **Look after your body, soul and spirit, by eating well, exercising, and caring for others.**

- **Obey the law.**

- **Respect others**

- **Only get what you need.**

PRUDENCE

- **Look after all that you have.**

- **Look after yourself.**

TEMPERANCE

TEMPERANCE

Temperance does not mean abstinence. Even though, Temperance Societies criticise excessive alcoholic consumption, or advocate a zero alcohol policy, it is not the technically correct definition for temperance. Excessive alcoholic consumption can lead to family breakdowns, ill health, loss of employment, and traffic accidents with consequential loss of your license and jail time. All these would have an impact upon your finances.

If you regularly attend parties and consume more than 3

TEMPERANCE

standard drinks of alcohol, then you are already drinking to excess. If you feel you need a drink to relax after work or to face a situation or to get you in the mood to meet up with friends, you have a drinking problem. Try having a 'dry week', then a 'dry month'. If you are unable to manage this without serious problems, or if you just cannot do that, you will need to seek help.

Temperance is moderation. This means having and doing a little bit of everything, but not too much of any one thing.

Playing on computer games is good for hand-eye coordination, but more than an hour a day is not good because it eats into time for far more important things. If you do this in excess, your family, study, and home maintenance will all suffer, not to mention the damage to your body from screen radiation and lack of exercise. You should impose restrictions and ask your family to help if you find it difficult to just walk away after an hour of playing.

Spending all day attached to your smart phone, waiting for updates on the various chat and social sites and posting photos of your lunch, rather than being in the moment and enjoying it with your friends and family is very destructive behaviour. The cost of these social networks it threefold. Firstly, there is the actual cost of your phone and internet usage, which is often high on mobile devices. Then there is the cost in losing connection with your real family and friends, because you aren't actually communicating with them while you

TEMPERANCE

are 'plugged-in'. Finally, there is the cost to your health which deteriorates as you get less sleep, or suffer from insomnia and the enormous amounts of radiation you expose yourself to. The World Health Organisation has listed the dangers of exposure to mobile device radiation www.who.int/mediacentre/factsheets/fs193/en.

Since 2014 all mobile service providers have been required to warn their mobile customers of the risks so that they can't be sued in future.

Try a week without checking out your e-mail, Facebook, Twitter, and Instagram accounts, and answer phone calls and say hello in person to your friends and family, unless you really need to use those accounts for your work. Now, if you cannot manage this without experiencing distress, you should seek help from Lifeline 13 11 14 www.lifeline.org.au or other similar counselling services which have been included at the end of this book.

Temperance means you exhibit self-control and do not explode when you are angry. You present your case in a calm manner and do not resort to abuse or violence. If others are intemperate simply move out of their way until they cool off.

If you have a dispute with your neighbours over fencing, trees, dogs, parties, loud cars, rubbish, or anything else. Just try calmly talking to them. Use words such as, "We have trouble sleeping when you have parties outside. Could you please move indoors and turn the music down after 9.00 pm?" If they are reasonable, and they probably

TEMPERANCE

will be, they will oblige. If a tree branch is bothering you, try "Have you noticed that your tree branch is breaking our gutter, would you like us to trim it back to the fence line? Or would you prefer to do it yourself?" In each case you should speak to the neighbour calmly when neither you are they are rushed, stating the situation, no accusations, no rudeness, no name calling or bad language. Generally your neighbour will be unaware of the effect their behaviour has and will remedy it. Occasionally it will not be possible to sort things out as simply as this, which is when it is wise to seek mediation.

The Queensland Government's Department of Justice and Attorney–General has an excellent website that will guide you through all sorts of disputes, explaining your legal position with you and your neighbours rights and responsibilities:

www.qld.gov.au/law/housing-and-neighbours/disputes-about-fences-trees-and-buildings.

If you find this a bit daunting just navigate around their site. You can read their publication about mediation at:

https://publications.qld.gov.au/dataset/17cb1543-c4af-495d-9412-f43f673dc79e/resource/050c6991-1e22-4933-b185-c92f770eb78a/download/neighbourhoodmediationkit.pdf

This mediation booklet gives excellent advice on

TEMPERANCE

handling discussions and preparation for solving disputes. It is well worth reading, even if you are not in dispute with anyone, as it includes good interpersonal skills. For example, if someone is very angry over your trolley in a supermarket, the simplest thing is to say, "Sorry" and move on. You may have done nothing wrong, or you may not be aware you blocked their way, but it instantly defuses the situation. Usually trolley rage has little or nothing to do with the supermarket, but a lot to do with how the person was feeling before they started shopping. If something fell down help to pick it up. Otherwise keep clear, and do not escalate the situation with accusations. Just calmly get out of the way.

Road rage is common. Do not do it.. Ever... Not for any reason. It does not help, and it only makes the situation worse, which could lead to loss of life or serious injury. Leave a minimum two-second stopping distance from the car in front of you. It is required by law, and specified on the Department of Transport's website:

www.tmr.qld.gov.au/Safety/Driver-guide/Speeding/Stopping-distances.aspx.

When others cut in, swerve between lanes, run red lights, or drive through give way signs without stopping, you will have a safe stopping distance to avoid an accident. Try not to be offensive if this happens to you. Stay calm, and remember you are driving a vehicle capable of killing someone. Also, do not let others in your car be offensive to other drivers. If someone wants to overtake you, let them. If someone cuts-in in front of you give

TEMPERANCE

them space. If someone notices too late where their turnoff is and swerves, give them room. Remember, one day it might be you in that situation. Try driving while listening to calming music and suck on a peppermint. You will be surprised how much better it will make you feel and you won't even find yourself bothered by other aggressive drivers on the road. Do not let the actions of someone else make you become a hazard on the road. It's a chain reaction. So, if one abusive driver upsets another driver, then you have two abusive drivers on the road, each of whom upsets even more drivers on the road, until every driver is abusive on the road. But all it takes is one single driver to remain calm to stop this chain reaction.

With illegal or "recreational drugs" there is no such thing, as temperance. Zero drugs is the only legal and safe choice for health, finances and freedom. Be aware that if you take illegal drugs you could still test positive to them, even six weeks after your last use. It's worth remembering, if you are driving in a manner which attracts the attention of police. They generally have a policy of testing for alcohol and drugs whenever they pull someone over for driving in a dangerous manner. If you value your license and your freedom don't take any recreational drugs.

Temperance

- **Moderation.**

- **Calm, restraint, self-control**

COURAGE, FORTITUDE

Courage is doing what you should do even though it is not easy. You need courage to stand up against what is wrong, especially if there are consequences if you do. Perseverance is sticking with a task until its completion, regardless of how difficult it is. The Australian poet, jockey and politician, Adam Lindsay Gordon, describes courage as:

> "Life is mostly froth and bubble,
> Two things stand like stone.
> Kindness in another's trouble,
> Courage in your own."

In your studies, perseverance is keeping up with all the study and research and course work, even if it means sacrificing most of your social life. That is the price of performing a good job (Short term pain for long term gain.) Courage is undertaking difficult academic work in order to achieve your long term goals. To endure all the effort and worry that you may not be able to complete something, your perseverance will see you through.

When it comes to facing financial hardship, courage and perseverance are irreplaceable. You require courage to face up to your financial problems and to start working on solutions. You need perseverance to do all the things that need to be done to get yourself out of debt. Initially, this will involve a harsh restrictive budget, self-control, and temporary denial of self-gratification. It will be painful, but worth it in the end. You should congratulate yourself for each little milestone. Take pride in your efforts, because soon you will be able to see the light at the end of the tunnel. Admitting your problem exists is often the most difficult part. Yes, admitting to others that you require a little extra time to pay your debts is embarrassing... Do it anyway! Soon you will no longer need to ask for extensions. Just persevere.

Get a mentor when you are studying. Hang out with people who help lift your spirits up and don't bring you down. However, you also have the responsibility of lifting other peoples' spirits up as well. Even when the going is tough, do your best and don't be afraid to ask for help. Most people are willing to help you.

Never be tempted to download or buy assignments online. The humiliation of leaving a University for dishonourable conduct is something you will live with for the rest of your life. You might spend the rest of your life wondering: "If only I had persevered, maybe I could have passed that difficult subject and graduated." Support and perseverance are the two things you require when facing any difficulties. My whole family celebrated when I received a pass in my most difficult subject. They still remember those celebrations, but none of them remember the subjects which I sailed through to achieve 100% with ease. My book, The Perfect Assignment, will show you how to do your research faster and more efficiently, this will give you more confidence and remove the need to cheat.

When it comes to your health, face up to issues such as the need to start an exercise programme, or needing to lose weight, like 60% of the Australian population. Accept that fact that you can do something about it. If you face eating issues associated with anorexia and bulimia, or have a problem with alcohol, or prescription or illegal drug abuse you can do something about it. If you smoke too much, or bite your nails, or inflict self-harm. You can do something about it. If you have an addiction to the internet, or viewing pornography, or gambling, or social media overuse. Remember, you can do something about it!

All you need is courage, to accept you have a problem and start doing something about it, and perseverance to continue the fight to get back in full control of your life.

All of these health problems affect your finances. You will have less to spend, share and save. You will become less efficient at work and require more sick days. Which means you are less likely to get promoted, which translates to less income or no job at all! You will also incur the additional cost of ongoing treatment. If you let your health issues get out of control, an early death is likely.

It is not considered polite to point out someone is overweight, so no-one will tell you that you're overweight. Weight creeps up slowly, so you do not notice those extra pounds straight away. Some stores make their sizes a little larger each year. This means, if you keep the same waist size, you go down a clothing size. Why do stores do this? I was told customers will not buy a garment, even if it's a perfect fit, if it means they need to buy a larger size. The stores need to make sales, so they change their clothing sizes. Some of the retailers use a specific group of people to set their garment sizes to. Then as these people and put on more weight the retailer adjusts the dimensions of their garment sizes accordingly. These retailers do not use a rigid standard size with set measurements for their garments. Ask yourself, "Am I able to grab a hand full of flesh at my waist?" Have you started buying larger size clothing? If you answered "YES" to any of these, it's time to see your doctor and ask if and how you need to lose weight. Crash diets are not a good idea. If you are obesely overweight you will require monitoring as you lose weight. Diabetes Australia has a very useful website for diet and health advice:

www.diabetesaustralia.com.au.

There is a quick way to determine if you drink too much alcohol. All you need to do is ask yourself, "Do I want this drink or do I need this drink?" If you feel you need a drink after a hard day, then you probably have a drinking problem. Do you drink every day? Do you drink to get drunk? To confirm if you have a drinking problem, try this: Try to see if you can do without a single drink for a whole month. Think of it as a "dry July", or any other month of the year. If you made it all month without a drink, well done. Otherwise it's time you got help. There are two organisations which can help you:

Alcoholics Anonymous, for those with drinking problems www.aa.org.au

Al-Anon for families of those with drinking problems www.al-anon.org/australia

If you need help facing problems of all sorts, call **Lifeline** on 13 11 14 www.lifeline.org.au. If they cannot help, they will put you in contact with the right organisation. Remember, they really do care.

If you find you are regularly spending money gambling, regardless of whether it is lotto, horses, dogs, sports bets, or the pokies (slot machines) and it's affecting your financial situation contact

Gamblers Anonymous. They will support, encourage and help you:

www.gansw.org.au

Courage

- **Facing your fears.**
- **Doing what is needed.**

Fortitude

- **Sticking with it, all the way through to the end!**

Chapter 3

SEVEN VICES

LUST

GLUTTONY

GREED

SLOTH

WRATH

ENVY

PRIDE

LUST

Attraction to your life partner is good. It is healthy and it keeps you together when life gets a bit tough, and should ensure you stay together to look after the next generation.

Googling sexually offensive material of any sort is wrong, because it puts a barrier between you and your

LUST

partner, and devalues your relationship. Storing, accessing or downloading specific sexually offensive material on your computer can be illegal, which would result in the loss of your Blue Card, which is necessary for many jobs, volunteering, and being a part of many social groups. It can also lead to prosecution, jail sentences and fines. Losing a Blue Card can prevent you from working at government departments or schools. A charge, regardless if you are convicted, would still result in all of the above, except for the jail time. It would also mean you would be denied a visa to many countries such as the United States, Singapore, and most Middle Eastern countries.

Value your partner by not spending time looking around to see if there are others who are younger, prettier, more handsome, wealthier, or better dressed. By honouring and valuing your life partner you will see them in a better light and appreciate them. The result will be that they will do the same for you. Be trustworthy and respectful.

Being faithful and loyal to your husband or wife will save the massive fractures caused by divorce. It also means your finances are stronger because your assets and attention are not divided.

Lust

- **Avoid pornography.**
- **No affairs.**
- **Be loyal in body, mind and spirit.**

GLUTTONY

Gluttony is eating too much, and buying too much to eat.

We have all piled our plate a little high at an all you can eat buffet at some time in our lives. There wouldn't be anyone who has not done that at least once. This is called gluttony, when we see all the wonderful choices and find it really hard to limit our choices. Just a tiny bit of all the things that you would like to taste soon add up to an enormous plate. The result is feeling over-full, indigestion and probably a restless night. Overindulgence like this, on a regular basis and calling it dinner, will result in obesity.

There are also more subtle forms of gluttony which sneak up on you. For example, if you are having a take away meal and you are asked if you want to 'up-size' or, worse still, 'super-size' for just a few cents more, it can be hard to say no. There is currently an obesity epidemic in Australia and many other developed countries in the world. Convenience foods are a major contributor, but mostly the problem is consumers' gluttony and lack of self-control.

You can easily avoid this by preplanning your food for the whole week and only buying what you need. Try packing your own lunch and restricting takeaway meals to an occasional treat only, such as less than once a month. Serving size can also be a problem when cooking your own meals. If your dinner plates are large do not put any food on the decorative section of your plate, or even better, try serving dinner on a bread and butter or dessert plate, if you are attempting to lose weight.

Not only does gluttony and obesity cost you money, it also has a negative impact on your health and self-esteem. Such health issues include: heart attack, stroke, high blood pressure, diabetes, cancers, sleep apnoea and arthritis, just to name a few. Treatment for all of these conditions is expensive, uncomfortable and these diseases can all become life limiting. Additionally, you will also need to spend money on a new wardrobe as your clothing size increases.

Gluttony

- **Do not eat or buy in excess.**
- **Plan your meals.**
- **Obesity can kill you.**
- **Treatment is expensive and unpleasant.**
- **Buying a larger wardrobe is expensive and not flattering!**

GREED

You do not need the latest computer when you can use the library computers for free. Your phone does not need upgrading if it works. You do not need Pay-TV, the programmes are similar to those on free-to-air anyway. You do not need take-way meals, just pack your lunch or eat at home. Your children do not need the latest toys and gadgets; they just need your love and attention. Join toy swaps and visit charity shops. You do not need brand name clothing, just be clean and neat.

GREED

The best way to avoid greed is to turn off your TV or do not watch the commercials. If something is being advertised to try to get you to buy it, it is something that you don't need. However, if you really need such an item, you should only buy it, if and when you have the money for it. You should not have to consider whether it is the latest model or if it was featured in a movie or whether a famous sports star uses it.

For example, if your jeans are worn out and there is not much cotton holding them together, you need a new pair. This does not mean that you need a specific brand; you just need ones that fit and suit the purpose. To purchase a new pair of jeans you could spend $7 in a discount chain store, or well over $450 for a designer pair in a classy boutique. Nobody 'needs' the more expensive one, but some may still desire it. Charity stores will often have the same $450 designer jeans for sale the next season for around $4. Only buy what you need and nothing more.

Show restraint with your 'toys' as well. To avoid impulse purchases, take time to think about the item. If you still want that item next month, and you can afford it, and you need it, and you have no pressing debts, then you can buy it or save up to buy it . When you do buy it, pay in cash and negotiate for the best deal. Once you have it, look after it, and do not replace it as soon as a newer model is released.

Despite what the advertisements tell you, you do not need a new look in your home furnishings each season. Only buy sheets, quilts, pillows, etc., as you need them, not just because you want a new spring look.

To save money on the things that you do need, such as clothes for growing children, buying out of season does make a difference. For example, at the end of winter buy winter clothes for the next year. Do the same for buying summer clothes at the end of the summer season. This will usually save you between 25% and 75%, and sometimes you will save even more. Remember to buy only what you need, and if you do not need it, then it is not a bargain at any price!

If you need to pay the rent, or a mortgage, you have a contractual obligation to do so. If you cannot afford what you have, it's time to downsize. Remember to live within your means. If you use electricity or gas you are paying for it, so do not waste it. This means not using air-conditioners when a fan will suffice, and turn off any unused appliances.

Greed

- **The most expensive may not be the best anyway.**

- **You do not need multiple items such as TVs or tablets.**

- **Do not spend what you do not have to buy what you do not need.**

GREED

- **Pay debts before treating yourself.**

SLOTH

Sloth is just plain laziness.

There is the laziness of doing a near enough job at work rather than a good job, which is a good way lose your self-esteem and your job. You should take pride in all the work you do. If someone is willing to pay you to do a job, they consider it worth doing. Therefore, you should do that job to the best of your ability.

There is the laziness of not checking if you are getting the best deal with your insurance or other regular accounts at their renewal time. Often rates increase, and if you are not taking notice, you can pay a lot more than you should. My car insurance is a perfect example. The premium increased from $260 to $450 with no explanation. All I received was a renewal notice. As soon as I noticed this, I contacted their competitors and ended up getting a much better deal. Then I telephoned my insurer to tell them I could get it cheaper elsewhere. It's no surprise that they happily matched the price of their competitors to keep me as a customer. I saved myself $190 with just two phone calls and 30 minutes total time spent being proactive. The same applies for the bank fees on your accounts. Check that you have the best accounts for your situation (i.e. no fees; no charges; and get them to pay you interest, not the other way round).

There is the laziness of not keeping up maintenance. The old adage of a stitch in time saves nine still holds true as ever. A little tear one centimetre long in your shirt will take 5 minutes to stitch up by hand by the most fumble-fingered person. However, if you ignore the tear, it can rip right through your shirt whilst you are wearing it. The shirt becomes a write-off and could leave you in an embarrassing situation. If you decide to leave the oil unchanged in your car, your car will soon have massive engine damage that could become more expensive to repair than a replacement car. The same goes for your washing and house cleaning. If you are renting and do not keep up with cleaning you can be landed with a rather large bill for professional cleaners when you move out. You could even be evicted and still have to pay for professional cleaners.

There is the laziness of not preparing your food or cleaning up afterwards. Buying take-aways or pre-packaged food is all right occasionally, but it is very costly to your budget and to your general health. Not cleaning up afterwards will lead to cockroach and vermin infestation as well as gastric stomach symptoms.

Also, there is the laziness of not doing assignments or the necessary preparation or study needed for work. The results of this are just too obvious... failure and limited life choices!

Sloth

- **Do your job properly.**

- **Check your accounts.**

- **Do maintenance.**

- **Prepare food properly.**

- **Do all the necessary study or preparation required.**

WRATH

Wrath is uncontrolled and vented rage. There are no excuses for road rage, trolley rage, domestic or public violence, and any other rage... Just do not do it! It is illegal, immoral, and causes so much damage to relationships, your employment, customer relations, and it often leads to worse forms of violence. Wrath is not to be mistaken for self-defence when you are being physically attacked, which is entirely different.

Even venting rage orally, referred to as verbal abuse, can destroy relationships and see you summonsed to appear in court, which could be the least of the problems you will experience. If your verbal abuse escalates into violence, how would you feel once you calm down and come to realise the damage you have caused to property and other people? What if it resulted in death or permanent disablement to yourself or someone else? Could you live with that? Can they? Now, was that parking space really worth someone losing their life over? If someone cuts in front of you in traffic, assume they did not see you, so let them in and forgive them. You have probably done the same to someone else without realising it. Don't have a heart attack over it. Do not let this incident ruin your whole day or worse still your life.

Some media personalities and sportsmen often let their rages get the better of him. It often costs them dearly in prestige and costing them millions of dollars in endorsement contracts each year.

If someone tries to provoke you, just walk away. If a situation makes you angry, just count to 10... or count to 1000 if you need to. Put yourself in the position of the person you are about to abuse. How would they feel about this? Are you absolutely sure that you are in the right? Could you have made a mistake? If you are in the right, you do not need to argue, but if you are in the wrong, you cannot afford to argue.

Wrath

- If you are right, you do not need to argue, if you are wrong, you cannot afford to...

- Road rage.

- Domestic violence.

- Anger that needs management.

- All are wrong

ENVY

Envy, like greed, is just wanting what you do not need. Envy is the desire to have something just because someone else has it.

iPhones, iPads, iWatches, Rolex Watches, a Lexus, a Lamborghini, in fact any luxury brand, are all marketed to incite the envy in people. The specific promotion of such products tells you that you are worth nothing, that you are no longer awesome, simply because you do not have one of these latest shiny new status symbols. It's irrelevant whether you need it or not, whether you can afford it, or whether it's appropriate for your usage. What if there is something cheaper, older, or entirely different that better satisfies your needs? Their promotion tells you this is not important. What matters to them is that you feel less of a person if you do not have it and that you get yourself into debt to make them richer.

If you like someone else's hairstyle, that's known as admiration. This is a good thing. However, if you feel the need to get the exact same style, regardless of whether it suits you, just because you want to be as awesome and accepted as that person, that is called envy. This is a bad thing, because being green with envy is not a healthy look. When it comes to style, slavishly copying someone else's image is not only expensive, but it will more likely lead to others ridiculing you behind your back instead of admiring you for the wonderful person you are.

"Keeping up with the Joneses..." is a popular term for envy. The sad thing about keeping up with the Joneses is that the people you are trying to impress usually don't notice, do not care, become envious themselves, or are laughing at your attempts of trying to climb the social ladder. So all that effort and expense you went to, to copy someone else was wasted.

Learn to compliment or admire the style of others and be happy for them. This is the way to achieve a greater state of happiness. You can only ever be a perfect 'you'. If you try to be someone else you will only be a shadow of the true person you try to copy.

Envy

- **Be an authentic person – be yourself.**

- **Compliment, but do not copy.**

PRIDE

"Pride goes before a fall," is often misquoted from the Book of Proverbs, in the Bible. It illustrates that if your focus is on yourself, as centre of the universe, you are likely to trip over the mundane.

Take pride in your work. Do it well, but listen to advice and be open to suggestions for improvement. Evaluate

PRIDE

the advice you receive, and if you feel that it might work for you, try it. Notice that I did not say, "do everything someone else suggests," especially if they have less knowledge about your situation. However, if the boss strongly suggests that you do something a certain way and you see some danger in doing it that way, point out your concerns. If s/he still insists that his way is better, do it his way as s/he will be responsible for the consequences. Make sure s/he puts it into writing first. Obviously, do not do it his way if it is a breach of the safety rules or if it's illegal. Put it in writing why you are disobeying his instructions. Do not let your pride stop you from trying it his/her way. You never know, you might find a better way or even learn a new skill.

Do not let your pride stand in the way of you apologising either. This is a sure way to destroy relationships. If you feel that you are even half wrong, apologise. Make reparation for any damage you have caused. Never expect forgiveness unless you are going to try to right the wrong you have caused.

Pride usually prevents you from listening to the educated and qualified advice of others. Lose your pride and start to learn. Always remember to evaluate the advice on the basis of who gives it, their experience, their knowledge, and whether they have your best interest at heart. Never, never accept advice and follow it blindly, which is just expecting others to take responsibility for your decisions. You are the only person responsible for your own actions, or lack thereof. I hope that you evaluate everything in this book, noting all that is relevant to you, and deciding what will work for you. Just because something is in writing or on the internet does not necessarily make it right.

Pride

- **Take pride in your work.**
- **Overcome pride to listen.**
- **Overcome pride to apologise**
- **Evaluate all advice.**

Chapter 4

EDUCATION

Focus on what you need to know and get qualified for what you want to do. If you are just going to university to get a degree because most jobs these days need a degree. STOP! Go and speak to trusted family members who know you well. Then speak to your older friends. Lastly, go and see the careers advisory service at your university. Do not be aimless. If you have no direction you will not get to where you want to be. Figure out your preferred career path, alternatives that interest you and where you would be willing to work. Find out the pre-requisites for each of these fields. Study all the required subjects to get the appropriate qualifications, and any extra subjects to get the required number should be those that you really love and could be successful in. Who knows they could even turn out to become a future career direction for you?

No learning is ever wasted. You never know when it will be useful. Focus on what you need to know first!

EDUCATION

Qualify yourself to support yourself and your family and then learn for your own interest.

Get a part time job and pay your HECS (Higher Education Contribution Scheme) fees or the equivalent in other countries, upfront. It will save you a minimum of 25% plus interest, and in some private colleges you can often save up to 50% off their education fees. Your part time job could even help you get the job you want. For example, if you are studying a veterinary medicine degree, and you work part time cleaning animal cages etc. at the local veterinary surgery, it makes it easier for you to get a practical placement. You might be paid as a qualified veterinary doctor before you even end up completing your final semester of study. Any related field also helps, as does office cleaning. Last time I checked, a night office cleaner was earning more than a full time teacher. With that sort of money you could pay for your education and have enough for a house deposit before you graduate.

Check if last semester's textbooks are the same as this year's. If they are, try to contact other students to buy the texts as secondhand. Later you can sell them again to recover the cost when you no longer need them. Use your student union card everywhere to get discounts. Look at performing arts websites; you can visit the opera, ballet and orchestra for as little as $25 while the other adults in the seats next to yours are paying hundreds of dollars to see the same event. A cultural education is as important as an academic one. Visit the state libraries, art galleries and museums, most are free,

EDUCATION

as are parks and most national parks in Australia.

Be the best qualified in your job. No job is ever 100% safe. Even the last pope retired a little early instead of dying on the job. If you take advantage of every educational opportunity that comes your way, and keep your skills up to date, you will show that you care about your work and not end up being easily replaced by someone who just became more qualified. You may have other qualifications and experience.

Learn extra to be considered for future promotions. If you aspire to be better or change what you're doing, you should plan ahead and get qualified. Studies that improve your knowledge of your current job are tax deductible. Ask others in your office, business, and workplace what their jobs entail. It is important when you need information to know who has it. Become qualified before you consider changing jobs. Do not leave a job unless you already have a new one to go to, unless your health or sanity are at risk at your current job.

You can learn a new skill or craft just because you can. It makes you feel good and slows the onset of dementia. Crafts and skills let you relax while producing something either artistic or practical in value. Feel the joy. Learn together with others and develop a new group of friends.

Education

- Focus on what you need.

- No learning is wasted.

- Upfront payment for you education is great.

- Save on textbooks.

- Be best qualified in your job.

- Learn for future promotions.

- Learn crafts and skills for fun.

Chapter 5

BANKING

Make the bank manager your friend. Your bank manager should know all the best promotions and interest rates. When you apply for a loan, and you are a loyal customer, that is taken into account. If you get into difficulties, you should get good advice. Shop around for the bank that suits you best. The big four banks in Australia may not necessarily be the best for you. With their large numbers of customers they often forget the individual. They almost never have the lowest interest rates. I have had accounts with all the big four banks over the years. Many have excellent staff, but the accounts that they offer are no longer suited to me. I love the personal attention of a small bank that knows who I am and has good accounts and services. Find out which is the best bank for you. Do not let laziness cost you money.

Get advice from banking staff on the best account for you. You may have always had a particular style of account, but there may be a better one to suit your needs. You may pay ATM fees if you visit other bank ATM

BANKING

machines. To your shock and horror, you may also have to pay for any transactions at your own bank's ATM and for any over-the-counter transactions. So speak with the banking staff to find the best account for your situation.

Get accounts with no bank fees, no account keeping charges and no ATM fees. Make sure you earn interest on savings, the more interest, the better. Also, make sure you do not get charged a fee to be served at the counter. You need to ask these questions. The fees and charges are listed in the Product Disclosure Statement, PDS that you will be given when you open an account. Make sure you read it and ask if they have alternatives that do not charge those fees or have different terms or conditions. If you don't ask, you can't expect to get a better deal.

You should have a credit card, so you have a credit rating for later when you need a loan for a house. Make sure you get a credit card with no annual fees, and 50 days interest free. If you have a good credit rating, get a credit card which includes free travel insurance if you plan to do any traveling.

You can compare credit cards in Australia at the following websites:

> www.creditcardfinder.com.au
> www.creditcard4u.com.au
> www.creditcards.com.au/compare

When choosing a credit card do your homework, visit the banks' individual websites as well. Some of the best cards are not listed on comparison websites as these websites do not receive commissions from those cards. I have decided to include the above three comparison websites, because they display some excellent choices, although they don't contain all available cards. For example, even though Australia's Bankwest won the best value credit card award three years in a row, the above websites didn't include those Bankwest credit cards or the Heritage Bank credit cards or many of the other smaller banks' cards. Obviously these banks and building societies keep their credit card rates low by not paying commissions to have them included in such comparison websites. Keep that in mind before you order anything directly from a comparison site. Remember, there is no free lunch, someone always has to pay.

Warning! *Never buy anything using your credit card that you do not have the funds to pay for before the interest free period expires.*

The interest charges are not just charged on the items you are gradually paying off, but you also lose the interest free rate for all future spending until the month after you have paid it off in full. The best way of keeping yourself in control of your credit card is by always paying its balance off in full each month. Otherwise, you will become a slave to your credit card as it controls your life. It is easy to lose track of your spending, so it's best if you do not use your credit card all the time.

Cards that earn points whenever you spend usually cost a lot of money in their annual fees. If you have one of these cards, make sure you really are getting value for money with the points you earn. As a rule of thumb, you would need to spend more than $2,000 a month on a card with a good loyalty scheme to just stay ahead of an annual $99 fee. If you can't afford to, or do not have to spend, or even need to spend that much each month, you should get a fee-free card without any rewards. Banks are a business; they need to make a profit, so if they are giving you rewards, find out how you are paying for them. Remember, there is no free lunch, someone always has to pay. If you intend traveling, make sure you get a card with free travel insurance included, which can be better than any travel insurance you purchase privately.

Debit and Pre-paid cards are excellent! They have all the advantages of using a credit card to pay for things, but you're using your own money. Hopefully earning you interest while it sits available on your debit account. The best advantage of using a debit card is that you cannot spend if you don't have enough money in your account. Be careful, because some banks will allow you to overdraw your debit account using your debit card and charge you a hefty fee for doing so. Check with your bank first to confirm if they do this. Visa and MasterCard cards are best because they are widely accepted and the fees charged to retailers are the lowest. American Express and Diners Club International have some wonderful rewards but have the highest annual fees and charge the highest merchant fees to retailers. Therefore, these cards are not widely accepted. Remember if you receive something for free, find out who is paying for it. It will usually end up being you.

Banking

- Make the manager your friend.

- Get advice on the best accounts for you.

- Have accounts with no bank fees, no account keeping charges, and no ATM fees.

- Make sure you get interest on your savings.

- Credit cards get one so you have a credit rating.

- Never buy anything on the credit card that you cannot pay for before the end of the interest free period.

- Cards that earn points when you spend cost a lot of money in annual fees.

- Debit and Pre-Paid cards are excellent.

BANKING TERMS-LEARN THEM

PDS, product disclosure statement: A dreadfully boring outline of all the terms used, all the fees, charges, interest, conditions. It is usually long and in small print.

BANKING

Read it! Read it carefully with a highlighter and get your banker to explain and write their explanation on the printout before you sign anything. Always get a PDS when you start an account, enquire about credit cards or apply for any loan. If you find something needs to change after you have read it for you to be happy, speak to your banker. You have a cooling off period with no penalty, find out what it is and use it if you need to get out of the agreement. Do not be lazy this must be read and understood.

Simple interest: If you borrow $100 at 10% p.a. simple interest, you pay back $110 at the end of 12 months. If you pay it back early, you still pay $110. If the interest on your savings account or term deposit is paid into another account you are getting simple interest. Get it paid into the same account so you get compound interest.

Compound interest: If you borrow $1,000 at 10% p.a. interest compounded annually, payable at the end of the term. Year 1 you owe $1,100, year 2 you owe $1,210, that is interest on your interest, year 3 $1,331, year 4 $1,464.10. Compare that to if it were simple interest, 4 years at 10% p.a. interest totals $400 plus the principal $1,000 would only total $1,400. (Credit cards and loans mostly charge compound interest.)

Fixed interest: is when the interest remains the same for the term of the loan or term deposit, regardless of market interest rate changes.

BANKING

Variable interest. Changes without warning, though you will be notified that it has happened, on your account or loan statement.

Personal loans: Used for a special purpose like a car or a computer. It is usually unsecured meaning that the item you purchased will not be repossessed if you fail to make the loan repayments. You do however lose your credit rating and they can take the contents of other accounts to pay it. They may even force any other assets you own to be sold off at a Bailiff's Auction, to recover the amount still owed on an unsecured loan or credit card. Read the PDS.

Secured personal loan: The bank owns the item you are buying until the final payment is made. You cannot sell it (the car etc.) without permission of the bank until the loan is repaid in full. They also usually attach extra terms and conditions such as the type of insurance and sometimes even the insurer.

Mortgage (dead pledge): This is used to purchase a home. The bank owns the home until the final payment is made. After that, you still need to pay the extra to have the mortgage released, (it was $110 when I last paid it). Banks like to discourage the release of mortgage saying it saves you time and money if you want another loan. That can be the case if you want to use that mortgage again to invest in other houses. However, it also makes it harder to shop around for a better deal. I just love that bit of paper that says I own my house! I also love being able to shop around for the best price!

Investment loan: Borrowing money in order to buy a business, invest in stocks and shares, or to purchase an investment property. The rates are usually higher than for a mortgage on the house you live in. The idea is you borrow to make more money. It works if you make money, but if the investment loses money or folds you have the loss plus you still need to pay off the loan with no income. The bonus is that the interest, fees and charges are tax deductible against the investment income.

Margin lending: The riskiest of all loans. The bank lends you money to buy shares and similar. They agree to lend say 50% of the market value. This is fine if the shares go up in value and you sell to make a profit and clear the debt. However, if the value goes down and the amount you borrowed is now 80% of their market value you have a 'margin call'.

Margin Call: This means you may have only 3 days to pay the difference to the lender to bring the loan back to 50% (which may involve you having to sell any other shares or assets you have to come up with the required money), or the lender will sell all your shares on margin loan to cover the debt. This means selling in a hurry with the shares going down further as others are probably in the same position. This can mean massive losses. If the sale of all the shares on a margin loan does not cover the debt, you will still owe money to the lender which needs to be immediately repaid. If you need to read this to learn about investing do not get a margin loan. While it

BANKING

is tax deductible, the chances are that after you have received a margin call you probably made a loss not a profit that year.

Chapter 6

Buying & Owning a House

Put aside at least 10%, or preferably 20%, of your wage to save up for a house deposit. If you are married you should also put aside all of your spouse's wage until you have accumulated at least a 20% deposit for a house. This will save you the 1.8% insurance and you also get a better interest rate. Apart from saving up for your deposit quicker, by putting aside all of your spouse's wage, if one of you ends up being out-of-work both of you are already used to living off one wage. This is also a good way to budget for maternity leave. You can pay extra off your mortgage very quickly using that second wage to save for investments and or holidays and education expenses.

What is Mortgage Protection Insurance? This is a policy you pay to insure your bank against your defaulting on your mortgage. You pay the bank's premium of 2.083% (correct on 16/07/2015), which is $6,250 on an average $300,000 home loan. If you default on your mortgage, because you become injured or lose your job, etc. they pay your bank. Their insurer then sells your house quickly at an auction without a reserve price for whatever they can get that day. Typically on a conventional loan, if your down payment (deposit) is less than 20 percent of the value of the home, lenders will require you to carry mortgage insurance.

Let's examine two scenarios where the insurer sells your house:

Scenario 1: Their auction of your house covers the mortgage and insurance debt:

You purchased your house for $200,000 and over the years you already managed to pay down your home loan, but you still owed the bank $100,000. Assuming your house had increased in value during those years and the insurance company was able to sell your house at auction for $210,000. From this sale amount, the insurance company will deduct their auction, advertising, stamp duty and legal fees. These could well be $40,000 to $50,000. They would also deduct the amount you still have outstanding on your mortgage in addition to whatever penalty fees are specified in your mortgage contract. This could all add up to around $180,000. When you deduct this figure from the auction sales price of $210,000, the remainder is only $30,000, which will be paid to you. Despite your having paid $200,000 plus interest all those years on your home loan, all you end up with is $30,000 and a really bad credit rating. Now you are going to have to find rental accommodation, which isn't going to be easy with a bad credit rating, depending on which Australian state you live in.

Scenario 2: Their auction of your house does not cover the mortgage or insurance debt.

You purchased your house for $200,000 but you have not paid down your home loan and you still owed the bank $200,000 at the time you defaulted, the situation is worse. Assuming your house had increased in value during those years and the insurance company was able to sell your house at auction for $210,000. From this sale amount, the insurance company will deduct their auction, advertising, stamp duty and legal fees. These could well be $40,000 to $50,000. They would also deduct the amount you still have outstanding on your mortgage in addition to whatever penalty fees are specified in your mortgage contract. The bank receives their money from the insurance company. However, you would now owe the insurance company $80,000, which you have to continue paying at unsecured interest rates that are much higher than your home loan rate was, and you're still going to have to find rental accommodation, which isn't going to be easy with a bad credit rating, depending on which Australian state you live in.

You may want to consider getting income protection insurance in case you become unable to work or lose your job, so that you can still continue to service your mortgage. For more on income protection read the chapter on Insurance.

BUYING & OWNING A HOUSE

Last century, people used to save up before buying a house, and usually bought a simple and affordable one. They then paid off their mortgage quickly. As their finances improved and their family increased in size, they would then sell their simple house and buy a bigger one. Unfortunately, young people buying houses these days seem to want to buy the type of house that their parents finished at when they retired, not the basic type that their parents started with when they were younger. This means the younger generation of today tends to over extend themselves when it comes to debt. Their attitude does not just end with buying their lovely big 'McMansion', they won't settle for just any old furniture for their new house, they insist it must be the newest and latest trend so they can show off to all their friends. This is a painful mistake which leads them to major stress and little joy as they face an almost insurmountable mortgage as well as furniture store and credit card debts.

You do not need a new lounge and furnishings. Charity stores and relatives who are downsizing have great stuff to give away. Consider this... When you start having children, they do not come 'house-trained'. They will have grubby hands, they will give you chocolate kisses, and at some time will probably vomit over your lovely white lounge. You might get a pet who will do all manner of naughty things to your lovely furniture whilst they are still becoming house-trained. Be realistic! Really nice furniture is bought when the children and pets are old enough to respect it. By that time you should already have most of your mortgage paid off and a little set aside for luxuries. Who knows, but you may have become attached to Aunt Lucy's lovely chintz lounge by then and not want a new lounge.

So that your house retains its value, make sure you keep up with maintenance and repairs. "A stitch in time saves nine," certainly holds true. Dripping taps cost you extra water and damage the bath or basin surface. Dripping gutters rot the timber supporting them. Peeling paint allows the surface underneath to degrade. Think of the memories created when working together to paint and decorate a bedroom. It costs just a small fraction of getting a decorator in. It will also be a source of pride for years. Your children, if they are old enough, will love to join in and help. That's entertainment, bonding, and maintenance, all in one!

Make your loan payments weekly, or at the very worst, fortnightly if you are paid fortnightly. Just doing this will cut years off your repayments and interest charges. You can have your monthly repayments automatically split in two, using your bank's online banking features, and paying your repayments twice as often. It's simple arithmetic, because there are 26 fortnights in a year, not 24. There are only 12 Julian calendar months in a year. However, there are 13, four week lunar calendar months in the year. Who would have thought all those left over days each month in the Julian calendar add up to an extra four weeks each year? By making 26 fortnightly repayments you will have just made an extra monthly repayment on your home loan. Get your bank manager to plug the figures into his computer to show you just how many years you cut off your home loan, and how much money you save. It is good fun!

Pay all tax refunds, and any overtime you earn, straight into your home loan. This is a really good idea, because the interest on your home loan is much greater than any interest you could earn on a term deposit or savings account. Because this is paid over-and-above what you are required, it comes straight off the home loan's principal, so there will be less interest to pay on your home loan in future. It's another win, win, situation.

Initially, when you start paying off a new home loan, most of your repayments are just going towards interest, with just a tiny bit reducing the principal. However, as time goes by and you pay more off your loan, a greater proportion goes towards reducing the principal as the interest component is less. That's the magic of compounding interest. Making extra repayments speeds this up. Interest on your home loan is calculated daily, so the quicker you repay the principal component, the better.

Get to know your neighbours. This is the greatest way to enjoy yourself and stay safe. Your neighbours can watch your place while you are out and you can reciprocate. When you have extra fruit you can share it with them. They will probably do the same, but even if they do not it is still good. If you remain respectful friends with your neighbours, problems do not get out of hand. This is the best insurance for your health and happiness, and it keeps your house safe too!

Negotiate for a mortgage with no fees and charges directly with the banks after checking all the websites first. Make sure you can get a home loan with no monthly fees, no start up fees and no penalties, if you pay it off early. Once you have found the best terms and conditions, get it emailed to you and take it to the bank that you prefer. The bank with service and people you trust. Then discuss what they can do for you, which includes all those terms or something better. Trust me, they can and will be reasonable. Because you will be paying $18,000 interest, 6% p.a. interest on a $300,000 mortgage, in the first year, they will want your money more than you need them. Remember, you are doing them a favour taking your business to them, not the other way around.

If you do not feel confident enough to do this yourself, get your parents to negotiate on your behalf. If they own their own home, their bank should be more compliant. Your parents should offer you moral support. Also the bank is more helpful to those with a larger nett worth. Being realistic, the banks want to keep their customers, including your parents. Helping their children would be a delight for most parents. They will probably be honoured that you asked them. When visiting your bank manager, your parents can also listen, as an extra pair of ears, and take notes and explain to you what is happening. Be aware, when all the details are being negotiated, it can be a little difficult for you to keep up with everything. If you are unsure of anything, always ask, and then ask again, until you are absolutely sure. Do not rush in, another perfect house will always come along.

Never use a mortgage broker. You will pay upfront and trailing commissions in addition to your loan interest. There is also a limited range of banks available to mortgage brokers, so it might not be the best deal for you. Remember what I said about credit card comparison sites? Someone always has to pay, and in this case it will be you. Let me explain... When you use a mortgage broker to get you the best deal in home loans, they can only access a limited number of banks, and almost all of the banks they have on offer are owned by one of the 'big 4' banks anyway. I am not aware of any of them that is not owned by one of the 'big 4', but I am sure that there must be some that are not.

The last time I helped someone who was using a mortgage broker to finance their home, they were charged $3,850 for an upfront fee, which was just added to their home loan. This means that my friends paid an additional 6% p.a. compounding interest on this amount over the whole life of their 30 year mortgage, which adds up to $23,247. Don't forget, there was still the trailing commission which was also added to their mortgage. My question is: "Why?" If you had only spent a morning checking out the various rates on your computer and chose a bank yourself, not only could you have had a better deal, but you would not have the burden of having to pay upfront and trailing commissions for using a mortgage broker. You could think of it as a laziness tax.

Have a mortgage offset account. Set it up as soon as you

get your home loan. This works by having all your income deposited into your offset account where it is available for you to use to pay all your bills. It works like this: If you have $1,000 in your offset account, you do not pay interest on that $1,000 on your mortgage. Since your home loan has a higher interest than you could earn on any savings bank account, you get a better interest rate on your savings which goes towards your mortgage, so your home loan gets paid off even sooner. You also do not have to pay tax on the interest earned as it is not paid to you. Instead it is paid off your mortgage. Win, win.

Do not get any other loan for anything until your mortgage is totally paid off. That's just plain and simple common sense. Do without, or save, but don't borrow. Do not overcommit yourself or you could end up losing everything.

Negotiate for a 25 year loan with no penalties for early repayments. Following this, you should pay it off in 10 to 15 years. This way you will not incur fees and penalty interest for daring to pay the money back early so that the bank can lend it to someone else. In my experience, most loans charge an additional interest charge equivalent to how much you would have paid had you not paid out early. For example, if you were paying $2,500 a month, cutting 10 years off your loan would save you $300,000 in repayments, or reducing it by 15 years would save you $450,000. Don't you just love it? It is enough to buy another house for the same price. Is it worth living having a more simple life whilst you are paying of your mortgage to get ahead faster? Or... Would you rather maintain your current lifestyle and struggle constantly to keep up the repayments? Avoiding the stress of not having enough money for the bills is surely worth a little belt tightening! You could purchase a rental property and allow the tenants the privilege to pay you rent, which you would obviously use to pay back that loan a whole lot quicker. Doing this I was able to pay back my 30 year investment loan in under four years, just by putting all the rental income towards the loan in addition to my income. The bank didn't believe it could be done, so they would not allow me to get a 10-year-loan, so I had to sign a 30-year-loan with no penalties. Not bad going for a person on part-time wages.

Buying and owning a house

- **Save a 20% deposit.**

- **Mortgage protection insurance – ouch!**

- **Buy where you can afford.**

- **Don't buy new furniture.**

- **Pay the loan weekly or fortnightly.**

- **Keep up with maintenance so the property retains its value.**

BUYING & OWNING A HOUSE

- Pay all your spare money into the loan.

- Get to know your neighbours; it is the greatest way to enjoy yourself and to keep safe.

- Negotiate directly with the bank to get a loan with no fees and charges, after checking all websites.

- Get your parents to negotiate for you if they own their home, their bank should be more compliant.

- Do not use a mortgage broker, you pay up front plus trailing commissions on top of your loan interest, there is also a limited range of banks available to them.

- Have a mortgage offset account.

- Do not get any other loans for anything until your mortgage is paid off first.

- Negotiate a 25 year loan with no penalties for early repayments, but then pay it off in 10-15 years.

Chapter 7

Debt Collectors

The best thing to do as soon as you realise you have trouble paying a bill is to contact the business as soon as possible, before the due date, to arrange a payment plan. Most businesses will allow you to do this and assist you with the process. However, don't expect any sympathy from them if you contact them after the bill is overdue.

If you have found yourself to be in the unfortunate situation where you have got yourself into financial difficulties and unable to pay your bills, you will probably be contacted by debt collectors. What is a debt collector? A debt collector is a person who collects on behalf of a business. In Australia a debt collector must hold a valid debt collectors license to do so.

As a consumer you have certain rights when it comes to debt collectors contacting you. These rights also extend to your spouse, partner, family members or someone else connected with you. A debt collector should only contact you when it is necessary to do so and when the contact is

DEBT COLLECTORS

made for reasonable purpose.

This includes:

- making a demand for payment
- making arrangements for repayments
- finding out why any agreed repayment plan has not been met
- reviewing a repayment plan after an agreed period of time
- Inspecting and recovering mortgage goods (only if they have a right to do so).

There are limitations to when and how many times a debt collector may contact you. A debt collector is only permitted:

- a maximum of three phone calls or letters per week or 10 per month.
- only allowed to contact you between the hours of 7:30 a.m. and 9 p.m. on weekdays, and between 9 a.m. and 9 p.m. on weekends.
- only permitted face-to-face contact with you between the hours of 9 a.m. and 9 p.m. on weekdays and weekends
- they are not allowed to contact you on national public holidays
- Debt collectors are not allowed to use extreme conduct, such as trespassing, forcing their way

DEBT COLLECTORS

into your home, or intimidation.

Here is a list of things a debt collector is not allowed to do at any time:

- They may not threaten to use any type of force towards you or a family member or any other person connected with you.
- They may not damage or threaten to damage any of your property.
- They may not block your way or block access to your property.
- They must leave when you ask them to.
- They may not trespass, such as enter onto your property when you have refused permission.
- They may not abuse you.
- They may not yell at you.
- They may not use racist or obscene language.
- They may not make demeaning personal comments about you.
- In the event that a debt collector has engaged in any of these prohibited actions you can immediately call the police, as they may face criminal charges. You should then also report them to the Australian Competition & Consumer Commission (ACCC).

Debt collectors are not allowed to take an unfair

advantage of you:

- If you are specifically disadvantage because of illness, age, disability, illiteracy or other circumstances.
  - If you are ignorant of the law.
  - If you do not understand the consequences of not paying your debt.
  - If you do not understand the debt recovery process.
  - Contact the ACCC to report such behaviour. The ACCC has the power to suspend a debt collectors license
  - If you have not agreed to the disclosure of your contact information, usually at the time you entered into a credit contract with the business you now owe money to, and they have forwarded on your contact details onto a debt collection agency, that business may be breaching the Privacy Act by disclosing your contact details to a third party without your permission. In this case you may wish to contact a lawyer for advice about suing the business for breach of privacy.
  - If you have already filed for a Declaration of Intention (DOI) to present a debtor's petition option, a debt agreement, personal insolvency agreement, or bankruptcy, all you need to do is give that bankruptcy number to the debt collectors the first time they contact you.

DEBT COLLECTORS

After which they must immediately leave you alone, and may no longer discuss the debt with you. They are no longer permitted to contact you regarding the debt. This is what is meant by bankruptcy protection. It protects you from debt collectors contacting you further regarding a debt. There are severe penalties for the debt collection agents and the business your owe money to if they continue to contact you regarding an outstanding debt after you have provided them with your bankruptcy file number.

For more information on your rights when it comes to debt collectors, refer to the ACCC website:

www.accc.gov.au/consumers/debt-debt-collection/dealing-with-debt-collectors

Chapter 8

BANKRUPTCY & OTHER DEBT OPTIONS

Assuming you have debt collectors knocking at your door, and you have absolutely no chance of meeting payments on a debt arrangement plan, and you are so deep in debt without any hope, you may feel that you need a new start. You may have heard of the term bankruptcy, but that's not the only alternative. There is also a declaration of intention, a debt agreement, personal insolvency agreement, and finally there is the dreaded bankruptcy. You should always consider bankruptcy as a last resort, because in ways it is similar to having a criminal conviction. It will prevent you from keeping or obtaining certain licenses for jobs such as security officer, real estate agent, financial planner, accountant, lawyer, being a Justice of the Peace, builder, and countless other professions.

During the period you are an undischarged bankrupt, you will lose the right to sue anyone, and you will not be allowed to leave the country (unless you apply for permission and permission is granted, which rarely occurs). You will not be able to hold any insurance, and you could end up voiding the insurance on any car you drive, and contents insurance in the house you reside in (even if the policy is in the name of someone else). Finally, you won't be able enter into any credit contract, which means you can't rent a car, apply for a post-paid mobile, home phone, or even rent a house in your name. Basically you're treated the same as a criminal would be. That's why the government came up with alternatives.

If you find yourself in financial trouble you can view options available to you on the following website:

www.afsa.gov.au/debtors/in-financial-trouble and watch their YouTube video

www.youtube.com/watch?v=7lQBuyKv6ic

The Bankruptcy Act provides the following four formal options to deal with unmanageable debt. The following are extracts from the Australian Financial Security Authority (AFSA) Personal insolvency information guide for debtors information booklet. You can download a Portable Document Format (PDF) version of the complete booklet here:

www.afsa.gov.au/debtors/personal-insolvency-information-booklet/personal-insolvency-information-for-debtors

Declaration of Intention (DOI) to present a debtor's petition option

This is an option under the Bankruptcy Act that provides temporary relief to allow you up to 21 days to decide whether to proceed with bankruptcy or another option. During the 21-day period, unsecured creditors cannot take any action to recover debts, including recovering money or seizing unsecured assets. In this time you can consider your financial circumstances, negotiate with your creditors and, where possible, make suitable arrangements to avoid entering a formal option under the Bankruptcy Act.

It is not recorded on the National Personal Insolvency Index (public electronic register of all personal insolvencies).

There is no fee to submit a DOI application.

You may lodge a DOI if: you have not applied for a DOI in the last 12 months; you have not signed a controlling trustee authority within the preceding six months (i.e. proposed a personal insolvency agreement to your creditors); you are not currently under a debt agreement, personal insolvency agreement or the subject of a current controlling trustee authority; a creditor has not already petitioned for you to be made bankrupt; you have a residential or business connection to Australia (i.e. you are living in Australia or conduct business in Australia).

Debt agreement

A debt agreement is a binding agreement between you and your creditors, where creditors agree to accept a sum of money that you can afford. Your repayments are based on your capacity to pay having regard to your income and all of your household expenses.

A fee is payable to AFSA on lodgment of a debt agreement proposal. Debt agreement administrators and other advisors may also charge a fee for providing information and preparing debt agreement forms. Funds received by an administrator are subject to a realisations charge (a government levy) which is paid by the administrator directly to the government.

Your name and other details appear on the National Personal Insolvency Index (NPII), a public record, for the proposal and any debt agreement.

Your ability to obtain further credit will be affected. Details of the debt agreement will also appear on a credit reporting organisation's records for up to five years - or longer in some circumstances.

During the voting period creditors cannot take debt recovery action or enforce action against you or your property; and must suspend deductions by such as garnishing your income.

You can lodge a debt agreement proposal if you:

- are insolvent (this means you are unable to pay your debts as and when they fall due);
- have not been bankrupt, had a debt agreement or appointed a controlling trustee under the Bankruptcy Act in the last 10 years;
- have unsecured debts, assets and after-tax income for the next 12 months all less than set limits. Limits are provided on the Indexed Amounts.

Personal insolvency agreement

A personal insolvency agreement (PIA) is a formal option available to help you deal with unmanageable debt. A PIA is a flexible way for you to come to an arrangement with creditors to settle your debts without being bankrupt.

It may involve one or more of the following, which will result in creditors being paid in part or in full:

- a lump sum payment to creditors either from your own money or money from third parties (e.g. family or friends);
- transfer of assets to creditors or the payment of the sale proceeds of assets to creditors;
- a payment arrangement with creditors (this could include deferral of repayments).

What are the effects of a PIA?

When you appoint a controlling trustee, you commit an 'act of bankruptcy'. A creditor can use this to apply to court to make you bankrupt.

Even if your attempt to set up a PIA fails, the appointment of a controlling trustee and the setting up of a PIA will still be recorded on the National Personal Insolvency Index (NPII) forever.

Your details will also appear on a record held by a credit reporting organisation for up to five years - or longer in some circumstances;

Once you have executed a PIA, you are automatically disqualified from managing a corporation until the terms of the PIA have been complied with.

You can propose a PIA under the following circumstances:

- you must be insolvent (this means to be unable to pay your debts as and when they fall due);

- you must be in Australia or have an Australian connection (e.g. you usually live in Australia or carry on business in Australia).

Bankruptcy

There are two ways you can become bankrupt:

1. **Presenting your debtor's petition**, referred to as voluntary bankruptcy:

If you are unable to pay your debts and cannot come to suitable repayment arrangements with your creditors, you may choose to voluntarily lodge a petition to become bankrupt (called a debtor's petition).

During and after your bankruptcy, you will face certain restrictions and have obligations placed upon you. You should read the information in AFSA's publication and seek clarification from a financial counsellor or contact us if anything is unclear.

If you decide to continue, you will need to complete and lodge a debtor's petition and a statement of affairs with AFSA within 28 days of signing the forms. Generally, debtor's petition and statement of affairs forms are processed within a 48 hour period. When the forms are accepted by AFSA you become bankrupt. You then receive a letter containing your bankruptcy number and outlining your duties and obligations whilst bankrupt. Please use your bankruptcy number whenever you contact your trustee.

You should carefully read AFSA's 'Essential bankruptcy information' which outlines what will happen to your assets, income etc. after bankruptcy.

The consequences of bankruptcy are serious and your bankruptcy cannot be cancelled if you change your mind.

2. A creditor (someone you owe money to) **makes an application** to court to make you bankrupt, referred to as involuntary bankruptcy.

If you are unable to pay your debts and have been unable to enter into an arrangement with your creditors and you haven't voluntarily made yourself bankrupt, a creditor to whom you owe $5,000 or more may apply to the court to have you made bankrupt.

Generally, the process for making you bankrupt begins when a creditor applies for a bankruptcy notice, and serves it on you demanding that you pay the money owed to the creditor within 21 days. A notice can only be issued if the creditor has obtained a court judgment against you within the last six years and the total amount owing under the judgment (or two judgments combined) is $5,000 or more.

If you do not pay the creditor by the time given in the notice, you commit an "act of bankruptcy." A creditor can then apply to the court (called a creditor's petition) to have you made bankrupt. The court gives you the opportunity to be heard before making the order. If after hearing the creditor's case and any submissions you make, the court is satisfied that you have not paid the creditor, the court makes an order (called a sequestration order) making you bankrupt. A trustee is appointed and you are then required to file a statement of affairs with AFSA within 14 days of being notified of the order.

Failure to lodge your statement of affairs is an offence under the Bankruptcy Act and you could be prosecuted.

If you do decide you wish to take up any of these options, **after you sought further advice,** you can find all the required forms on the following link:

www.afsa.gov.au/resources/forms/forms-for-debtors

Further information can be obtained by: contacting AFSA on 1300 364 785, visiting www.afsa.gov.au, or discussing your financial affairs with a financial counsellor.

Chapter 9

INVESTING

After paying off your home loan you might decide you want to invest in a rental property or in shares that you consider to be very safe. There are plenty of high risk alternatives, most of which are heavily advertised. Choose whatever you feel most comfortable investing in. You could also contribute a little extra into your superannuation. Check the current rules as they change so quickly. The advisers of your superannuation fund can provide you with advice. You could also visit an independent financial planner or the financial planner in your bank. Evaluate their suggestions and ask what commissions they are paid for each strategy. Determine if their recommendations are chosen for your benefit or theirs. There are many good honourable financial planners. Check their credentials, and watch out for 'cowboys'. As soon as cowboys are charged, they are removed from this list, some sooner.

To locate a certified financial planner and more tips on what to ask them at your first meeting you can visit consumer page of the Financial Planning Association of AustraliaLTD at www.fpa.asn.au.

INVESTING

Rental Property

When you purchase a rental property, make sure you are willing to live in it, otherwise how do you expect others to pay you to rent it? There is a main residence exemption rule where you do not have to pay capital gains tax on the sale of a property that was originally your main residence but you later decided to rent it out to tenants. A brief outline of the main points of this rule can be read at:

www.momentumwealth.com.au/property-tax-tips-capital-gains-tax-cgt-main-residence-exemption

Always check with your tax advisor first for more details and any recent tax law changes. Treat your tenants the way that you would like to be treated. Maintain your rental property so it retains its value and is fit for renting. Maintenance expenses are tax deductible and other improvements can be depreciated over time. Get yourself a property manager to make sure the rent gets paid. You should also get landlords' protection insurance (links available at the end of this book). Make sure that the rental income covers the loan repayments, or a little more, if possible. Negotiate the loan for a longer term if necessary so that it is affordable. Learn the rights for tenants and for you, as property owners.

For Queensland properties the Residential Tenancies Authority provides two information booklets which you can view:

INVESTING

Rights and obligations of landlords:

www.rta.qld.gov.au/~/media/Publications/Publications%20for%20managers/RTA_Managing%20general%20tenancies%20in%20Queensland.ashx

Rights and obligations of tenants:

www.rta.qld.gov.au/~/media/Forms/Forms%20for%20general%20tenancies/RTA-pocket-guide-for-tenants-house-and-units-form-17a.ashx

Similar information is available for other states and countries, on the web.

It never hurts to have a box of chocolates with a little welcome note waiting for your new tenants when they first move in, they then are more likely to respect you and the property, no guarantees of course.

Rental property

- **Buy only what you would live in.**

- **Maintain it!**

- **Use rent to pay it off.**

- **Use a property manager.**

- **Insure it.**

INVESTING

Shares

Before buying ANY shares consider this:

- Do I use their products or services?
- Is the company ethical? (They can incur big losses if they have to pay restitution.)
- Are they financially sound?
- Are they value for money?

Do your research. The Australian Securities Exchange (ASX) contains a wealth of free information, so make use of their unbiased website: www.asx.com.au. You could also sign up for an online stock broker. Most have a wonderful array of tools to help you and a help line if you are not sure or are lost.

Shares you could start with can be 'blue chips' such as banks or industrials in the top 100 companies. It is also fun to get shares for .001c each, where tiny changes can make big profits and or big losses, but do not limit yourself to only having them. Subscribing to various share and money magazines will give you a good idea of how you should approach investing in shares. Read at least two issues before you invest for the first time. Never borrow to buy shares. Once you have saved up a spare $500 that you do not need to pay bills you can buy shares with it. You build up your share portfolio slowly. Gradually get a spread across all sectors: banking, mining, retail, commodities, and biotech. However, if you borrow to invest in shares, you could end up with nothing if there is another stock market crash. Such margin loans could make you massive profits, but it comes with a very high risk. You would still end up owing the money you borrowed, which needs to be repaid.

Re read margin loans and margin calls that I have copied here.

Margin lending: The riskiest of all loans. The bank lends you money to buy shares and similar. They agree to lend say 50% of the market value. This is fine if the shares go up in value and you sell to make a profit and clear the debt. However, if the value goes down and the amount you borrowed is now 80% of their market value you have a 'margin call'.

Margin Call: This means you may have only 3 days to pay the difference to the lender to bring the loan back to 50% (which may involve you having to sell any other shares or assets you have to come up with the required money), or the lender will sell all your shares on margin loan to cover the debt. This means selling in a hurry with the shares going down further as others are probably in the same position. This can mean massive losses. If the sale of all the shares on margin loan does not cover the debt, you will still owe money to the lender which needs to be immediately repaid. If you need to read this to learn about investing do not get a margin loan. While it is tax deductible, the chances are that after you have received a margin call you probably made a loss not a profit that year.

Shares

- **Learn about them first.**

- **Do your homework.**

- **Do not borrow for high risk, if inexperienced, or invest what you cannot afford to lose.**

- **Start small and build up.**

- **Invest in a spread of sectors.**

Superannuation

Superannuation is a form of saving for your retirement. Many superannuation companies include insurance policies within their products to insure for unemployment, sickness injury and even death. Check what you are covered for and what you really need. Policies within superannuation are often more cost effective than those outside, however make sure it is right for you. Obtain a copy of the PDS and read it with a highlighter. If there is anything that you are not sure of phone their help line and ask those questions. It is too late to find out after you need to claim that it was not the right policy.

INVESTING

In Australia it is compulsory to save into superannuation, the percentage of salary changes regularly so look up what is required on a government website and make sure your employer is paying in the correct amount. Also check on how it is invested and whether it is right for you. Ask questions, get replies in writing.

Salary sacrifice to increase your superannuation. The following calculations are based on the 2015-2016 financial year for Australian residents:

Scenario 1: $0 to $18,200 assessable income, plus reportable employer super contributions, plus reportable fringe benefits.

This person only benefits from the first $1,000 from salary sacrificing per year because they are in the tax-free threshold. If they did make a voluntary contribution (e.g. salary sacrificing) they would pay 15% tax on that contribution, but benefit from the 50% government co-contribution up to $500 per year. By salary sacrificing $1,000 their super pays $150 of this amount to the tax department, and they receive an additional $500 from the government which is added to their super. That's a 35% return on investment.

Scenario 2: $18,201 to $37,000 assessable income, plus reportable employer super contributions, plus reportable fringe benefits.

INVESTING

This person saves 4% tax from salary sacrificing on the first $18,799 per year because they are in the 19% tax threshold, and super contributions are only taxed at 15%. If their income is below $35,454 they still benefit from the 50% government co-contribution up to $500 per year, but this amount reduces to $300 if their income is above that amount.

Scenario 3: $37,001 to $80,000 assessable income, plus reportable employer super contributions, plus reportable fringe benefits.
This person saves 17.5% tax from salary sacrificing as long as their total super contributions (including the compulsory 9.5% employer contributions) do not exceed $30,000 per year because they are in the 37% tax threshold, and super contributions are only taxed at 15%. If their income is below $47,454 they still benefit from the 50% government co-contribution up to $300 per year, but this amount reduces to $100 if their income is $50,454. Above this amount there is no government co-contribution.

Scenario 4: $80,001 to $180,000 assessable income, plus reportable employer super contributions, plus reportable fringe benefits.

This person saves 22% tax from salary sacrificing as long as their total super contributions (including the compulsory 9.5% employer contributions) do not exceed $30,000 per year because they are in the 37% tax threshold, and super contributions are only taxed at 15%.

INVESTING

Scenario 5: over $180,001 assessable income, plus reportable employer super contributions, plus reportable fringe benefits.

This person saves 32% tax from salary sacrificing as long as their total super contributions (including the compulsory 9.5% employer contributions) do not exceed $30,000 per year because they are in the 47% tax threshold, and super contributions are only taxed at 15%. With the beauty of compounding interest you will be responsibly saving for your retirement. The pain free way. There is no benefit on salary sacrificing more than the above amounts, unless you fall into a special category dependent on your age and the bring-forward rules. The above scenarios are only to help explain the concept and you should always seek advice from your tax agent for your specific situation.

Superannuation

- **Check the current rules.**

- **Contributing small and often will provide long term gains.**

Chapter 10

BUYING THINGS

First ask, do I need it? Will I still want it next month, next year? Can I afford it?

Save up, pay cash and negotiate to get the best deal, get the best quality that you can afford and look after it.

Whenever I ask for a discount I am usually offered a 10% discount or better. Some stores are apologetic that cannot offer you more than a 10% discount. When I compare the discounted price that I negotiated, it can be half the cost of buying it using my credit card and paying interest. But, if you buy it using your credit card and only pay off the minimum monthly amount, it will cost you more than 4 times what it would have cost had you paid cash for it and were offered a discounted price.

When you purchase a new car the upfront cost of paying for it is 60% less than if you had taken out the dealer finance with interest and paid it off over the next four to five years. Dealers earn most of their money on their finance loans, not the actual car sale, so it's no wonder they try to convince you to buy the car on finance. I just recently purchased a car, for cash of course! Naturally, the dealer offered it to me with finance. When I did the maths I decided to negotiate a better deal for purchasing the car with cash (or a bank cheque). The car salesman was genuinely lovely and very earnest. However, I got all the details and took them home to study before making my decision. Never buy anything on-the-spot on impulse!

With everything that you buy make sure you look after it, otherwise it is a waste. This applies to everything, from storing food correctly, to regular car services. It is always cheaper to maintain than repair or replace. When you purchase something, make sure you factor in their regular service costs, to know if you really can afford it.

Buying Things

- **Save up.**

- **Pay cash.**

- **Negotiate for the best deal.**

- **When purchasing a new car you save 60% by paying cash upfront compared to getting dealer finance over 4 to 5 years.**

- **Look after it.**

Chapter 11

MOBILE PHONES

Buy what you need, not what you think is cool. If you just need a phone to send and receive calls or send and receive SMS messages, and maybe even take the occasional happy snap, you just need to get a basic mobile. If you can get one that is 'unlocked' you will be free to choose from any network provider (e.g. Telstra, Optus, Vodafone, Virgin Mobile, Aldi Mobile, etc.) that has the best plan to suit your needs. You can also decide whether to prepay or post pay, have a plan or pay as you go. If you already have a tablet or a computer you really don't need to have internet on your phone for private use. Usually your employer should provide you with a phone capable of measuring or processing payments if you require it for your job. Remember: Get what you need. If you need it then get it, otherwise don't.

If you have relatives and friends overseas who you need to regularly communicate with, get a sim card for phoning overseas and swap it when needed. Otherwise, get a $29 phone for just the overseas calls. Some

MOBILE PHONES

companies advertise 1 cent a minute to India, and 2 cents for 5 minutes to China. Your local Indian store, or markets in Chinatown are the best places to get these.

To look for the best plans, try companies like Amaysim, Dodo, iinet, etc. for no frills. You will need to check their coverage though. In some country areas there is reception for only one network. If that is the case for where you live, make sure that your discount provider uses the Telstra network.

There are two other phone alternatives which most people don't know about. Firstly, if you have an Apple iPhone and your friends also have Apple iPhones, and both iPhones have FaceTime enabled, you can both call each other using FaceTime audio for free regardless of where you are in the world. (In this case you will need some data on your mobile plan, or if you connect your iPhone to your home wi-fi, then you don't need any data on your mobile plan.)

The second way to call people on your mobile is to register with a VoIP provider by installing their mobile app on your internet enabled iPhone or Android mobile. You can compare all the VoIP providers at the following website: www.voipchoice.com.au . Now you can use the internet to make any phone calls to any phone or mobile in the world at a much lower rate, and in some cases even free. For example, Engin currently has monthly rates ranging from $9.95 per month to $29.95 per month for unlimited calls (www.engin.com.au). The important thing to remember if you use VoIP to make all your

MOBILE PHONES

phone calls is that you no longer need to have calls included on your mobile plan, because you only want to use data. You can use VoIP regardless of the country you are in or mobile provider you are with. Telstra usually has the best coverage, and they have a prepaid sim plan called Mobile Broadband Plan, which gives you 12 GB of data for use up to 12 months currently retailing at $180. The only requirement is that you will need to own your phone outright to use this prepaid plan. Therefore if you use VoIP for all your calls you shouldn't be paying more than $180 a year for your mobile phone plan, unless you start using your mobile data up for silly things such as streaming movies.

Telco's prefer you buy a phone on a plan instead of outright so that you cannot take advantage of these cheaper alternatives. If you do your maths you may realise you may still be better off paying for your phone outright on a credit card on a cheaper prepaid plan than signing up for a postpaid plan over 24 months where you pay off your mobile.

If you do not really need internet or plan to use VoIP do not get it. Talk to your friends face to face and not in chat rooms. Remember to be careful with what you post on social media (Facebook, Twitter, etc.) as it affects your employment opportunities and your life. Remember: people do check! I have heard of many employers who check social media pages of all their prospective employees before deciding who to interview. Also you might not realise that Facebook installed on your mobile is the single greatest drain for your mobile phone battery. If you find your phone's battery life does not last long enough, try uninstalling Facebook. You can still use Facebook on your computer at home.

When traveling overseas, turn off your phone's internet, if you have it. Instead, use free wi-fi hotspots. Remember just don't use free public or internet at hotels to check your banking or make any credit card payments, as these are all vulnerable to hackers. It just needs one hacker to be connected to the hotel's wi-fi in any room in the hotel to be able to access your computer, tablet or mobile connected to the same wi-fi. There is a 98% chance of your credit card or passwords being intercepted when you are connected to public or hotel wi-fi. You can overcome this security issue by using a Virtual Private Network (VPN) on your mobile device. Put simply, a VPN just encrypts everything that your phone is sending or receiving over the internet so that hackers can't intercept it. One of the easiest ways to install it is by installing the OpenVPN app on your mobile:

> **For iPhones:**
> http://itunes.apple.com/us/app/openvpn-connect/id590379981?mt=8

> **For Android Mobiles:**
> http://play.google.com/store/apps/details?id=de.blinkt.openvpn

Then open the app and register as a new customer with

MOBILE PHONES

your email address, and follow the instructions on the screen. It is easy to install. Then enable it and you should see VPN somewhere on your phone's screen when it's enabled.

Internet on mobiles can cost many times that of home connections, so when at home connect your mobile to your home wi-fi. Check global roaming costs before going overseas. Telstra automatically activates all mobiles for use overseas. Some people return home to a surprise phone bill of over $10,000 for just a week in Bali. Leave global roaming off, turn data off, check up with email at free wi-fi hotspots. The internet is overflowing with stories of unsuspecting people being charged obscene amounts for global roaming due to data usage.

www.news.com.au/technology/australian-travellers-slugged-30-times-more-to-use-smartphones-overseas-with-competition-laws-stalled/story-e6frfrnr-1227413238654

Alternatively, if you have an unlocked mobile phone, then consider buying a pre-paid sim card for use overseas, which is much cheaper to use than international roaming, especially with VoIP or FaceTime audio. Experience your holiday, don't tweet it or you will miss the fun!

Mobile Phones

- **Get what you need, not what you think is cool.**

- **Look for the best plan, no frills.**

- **If you do not really need internet do not get it.**

- **Talk to your friends in real rooms not in chat rooms.**

- **If you own your mobile you are able to consider a VoIP plans.**

- **If you have an Apple iPhone you can take advantage of FaceTime audio calls.**

- **Be careful with what you post on social media sites.**

- **When traveling, turn off all internets if you have it, use free wi-fi, or buy a pre-paid sim card overseas.**

- **NEVER access your bank accounts or pay by credit card on public or hotel wi.fi, unless you use a VPN.**

Chapter 12

WEDDINGS

My mother had this sage advice for anyone who was going to get married...

BEFORE you get married each partner should save up six weeks wages and each person should keep it in a bank account in their own name (that the other partner can't access), and call it the DIVORCE ACCOUNT. You should never use this account except for its designed purpose (a divorce). If you every need to dip into it for an emergency, make sure you can replenish it in full within 6 weeks. If you can't replenish it in full then it is better if you do not touch it at all.

Her advice is still valid today as it was back in the 1970's.

There are three good reasons for having a divorce account:

1. If your spouse dies, all joint bank accounts are often frozen for six weeks or longer as the deceased estate goes through probate. You can't access any money

that is in joint accounts or in your spouse's name during that time.

2. If you are in a violent relationship this account allows you to get yourself and your children to safety. You will not be financially bound to stay with an abusive spouse.

3. Knowing that you are financially free to leave means you are more likely to be able to sort out your problems as you know you have options and do not feel trapped. Being trapped or feeling trapped is a definite relationship destroyer.

Divorce is not to be taken lightly. Marriage is a commitment, so when you separate you will feel that you have lost part of yourself. That said, if there is ANY VIOLENCE or ABUSE, GET OUT, GET OUT FAST and DO NOT RETURN. Remember, if violence happens once, it will happen again and more likely escalate than stop. Where there is no respect, there is no relationship! Seek a safe haven and change your phone number and e-mail address, stop using social media sites where your ex-spouse can track you down, and keep yourself safe.

I saw some frightening statistics in the paper this year. Did you know that the average wedding now costs between $10,000 and $50,000? Most of them being closer towards the $50,000 mark. What a waste! That $50,000 could be used as a substantial deposit on a house! The marriage and public commitment is

WEDDINGS

important, but the frills of a flashy wedding are not.

Before you even decide to consider jumping into marriage, or contacting a marriage celebrant or church, you should take the time to look at the following Queensland Government webpage on marriages, so that you know what is expected of you and what steps are involved in getting married:

www.qld.gov.au/law/births-deaths-marriages-and-divorces/marriage-weddings-and-registered-relationships/getting-married/

The average marriage celebrant (for civil weddings) charges between $500 to $1,350 for just their services, then there are all the other costs of hiring a venue and catering to consider. Here is a list of registered marriage celebrants in Australia:

www.celebrations.org.au/ceremonies/134-fast-find-a-celebrant/1652-regions

If you are planning on having a church wedding, hire the hall and self-cater or get the church ladies to do it for a small donation. Only invite close relatives and your closest friends. Do not invite people just because you feel you need to because they will not care if they are or are not invited anyway. Borrow a wedding dress or make your own or buy one on the internet. Remember you will only wear it for a few hours. Instead of presents that you do not need, especially if you have been living away from home for a while, ask for "bricks to build

WEDDINGS

your house" or for help with the honeymoon. Consider the idea of having a wedding in the botanical gardens and a share picnic afterwards. Be creative... Do not be wasteful! One of the saddest things I recently heard was about a couple having waited until their child was already able to walk down the aisle with them by the time they saved enough to have a wedding.

Not sure about getting married yet, but still want some formal recognition in your commitment to your partner until you decide to get married. Most people don't know that Queensland residents have the option to consider registering their relationship, with the Department of Births, Deaths and Marriages, by simply completing the form below and signing it in front of a Justice of the Peace instead. It's free and much easier to terminate than a messy divorce process. Then if you decide to get married later, your marriage certificate replaces the registered relationship certificate. You can download the application forms and information here:

Form to register a relationship (both people):

https://publications.qld.gov.au/dataset/8f1d4035-229e-4870-822e-baa63a59eb8b/resource/c6947b49-3c4d-4698-80cb-f6dda18abaf6/download/registeracivilpartnershipsubmission.pdf

Form to terminate a relationship (both people):

https://publications.qld.gov.au/storage/f/2014-04-17T00%3A55%3A49.736Z/application-to-terminate-a-registered-relationship-form-18.pdf

Statutory declaration to terminate a relationship (single person):

https://publications.qld.gov.au/storage/f/2014-04-17T00%3A58%3A24.768Z/registered-relationship-termination-statutory-declaration.pdf

Weddings

- Each partner saves six weeks wages in their own divorce account.

- If there is any violence, get out fast, and do not return.

- Instead of a flash wedding, put the funds towards a house deposit.

- Queensland residents have the ability to register a relationship instead of getting married, if they wish.

Chapter 13

DIVORCES

A staggering 27.6% of marriages in Australia ended in divorce in 2011, according to the Australian Bureau of Statistics. Divorce would likely have the biggest impact on your finances. Has your marriage broken down irrevocably? Are you sure you are not just experiencing the well-known seven-year-itch that almost all married couples experience? Psychologists call this the decline in happiness in a relationship after around seven years of marriage, also known as the end of the honeymoon period, where each person in a couple struggles to hold onto their identity as they notice themselves becoming bonded together as one person. Sometimes this causes feelings of resentment against the other spouse. Or are you or your spouse experiencing a mid-life crisis, the phase in our development that is experienced at some time between 40 to 60 years of age. During this time your spouse may show feelings of resentment towards you. There is no need to end a marriage for something that will only be temporary.

That said, if there is ANY VIOLENCE or ABUSE in

your marriage, GET OUT, GET OUT FAST and DO NOT RETURN. Remember, if violence happens once, it will happen again and more likely escalate than stop. Where there is no respect, there is no relationship! Seek a safe haven and change your phone number and e-mail address, stop using social media sites where your ex-spouse can track you down, and keep yourself safe.

Before you consider a divorce you may want to watch the movie War of The Roses with Michael Douglas, Kathleen Turner and Danny DeVito. It's about the best way to explain to you just how ugly and painful divorce will be. Make no mistake, there is no such thing as a nice, clean, and easy divorce! Your friends may tell you that, but that's not what they experienced. When something is so emotionally painful, most people live in denial and try to forget all the pain of the divorce process, and so they tell you it was fine, just because they forgot all the details.

The first thing you need to know about getting a divorce is that according to Australian law you can't get a divorce within the first two years of getting married. Assuming you have been married for more than two years, you will need to be separated for at least 366 days before you can even apply for a divorce. Then if your divorce is a simple case without child custody or complicated assets you will need to wait at least 12 months before the court can hear your divorce case, if it is filed with the Federal Circuit Court of Australia, which handles only simple divorce cases. Otherwise, for more complicated divorce cases filed with the Family Court of

DIVORCES

Australia (or Family Court of Western Australia for those living in W.A.) there is a three year wait until those courts can hear your divorce case. Most people who file their own divorce paperwork for simple divorce cases mistakenly file it in the Family Court instead of the Federal Circuit Court, which results in an unnecessary three year delay in their divorce case being heard. So one way or the other, from the day you separate to actually getting your certificate of divorce ('decree nisi') will take between two to five years, if all things go well. But if you make a mistake on your divorce application the wait period starts all over again!

Things you need to consider in divorces include: child custody; child support payments; splitting assets; what happens if there is a mortgage on the house; what if the sale price of the house is less than the mortgage; what about your joint bank accounts and credit cards being frozen; and your superannuation funds could be seized by your spouse as part of the divorce.

If you do decide to get a divorce, this is when you will need to rely on the savings you put into the divorce bank account you started before you got married.

You can download and use these fact sheets and divorce application forms. The divorce application fee alone is $845, and then depending on your circumstances, there are also daily hearing fees, subpoena fees, setting down fees, response fees, initiating application fees. NOTE: if you both fill out the divorce application as a joint-application, neither of you will need to appear in court:

DIVORCES

Divorce Fact Sheet:

http://www.familycourt.gov.au/wps/wcm/connect/36763cca-8b01-4f40-9e7e-f8e2e590189f/Preparing_affidavit0313V2.pdf?MOD=AJPERES&CONVERT_TO=url&CACHEID=36763cca-8b01-4f40-9e7e-f8e2e590189f

Application for divorce kit:

http://www.familycourt.gov.au/wps/wcm/connect/d9c6e4be-3288-4fc5-9080-e0ffb759beee/Divorce_Kit_0313_V3a.pdf?MOD=AJPERES&CONVERT_TO=url&CACHEID=d9c6e4be-3288-4fc5-9080-e0ffb759beee

Divorce service kit:

http://www.familycourt.gov.au/wps/wcm/connect/6bca8754-d4e7-4147-8929-7432f59e3d75/Divorce_ServiceKit_0313_V2b.pdf?MOD=AJPERES&CONVERT_TO=url&CACHEID=6bca8754-d4e7-4147-8929-7432f59e3d75

Thinking of using a lawyer instead? Consider this... Lawyers just love divorce cases, because the longer the case drags out, the more of your money they earn. If you need to use them, know what to expect, so don't make the divorce difficult by dragging it out. There may be nothing left for you or your spouse.

Divorces

- **If there is any violence, get out fast, and do not return.**

- **Divorces usually take between 2 to 5 years, or longer.**

- **Divorces are ugly, painful, and the biggest hit to your finances.**

- **If self-filing a simple divorce application file it in the Federal Circuit Court of Australia to reduce waiting time.**

- **If you both fill out the divorce application as a joint-application, neither of you will need to appear in court.**

- **This is where you will need to rely on your divorce account.**

Chapter 14

RETIREMENT

This is my favourite part. If you have been responsible during all of your life and followed this book, even if you have experienced a few global financial crises and a few dishonest real estate agents who took you for a ride, as we did, you should still be able to retire and be self-supporting when you decide to. We did. I retired at age 55 and my husband at age 62, because we wanted to travel.

When planning for retirement you need to assess the type of lifestyle you want. Visiting a financial planner to discuss your options with your super fund is a good idea when you reach this stage in your life. If you want a new car every 3 years, you will need to include it in your savings and calculations. It is a good idea to plan ahead. If you want to retire at 55 make sure you prepare a financial strategy with a financial planner well before you turn 50.

Before you retire get your home set up to be low maintenance. Get the painting done just before you retire, declutter, remove loose mats, fix anything that has been ignored and left for some day. At retirement age your body will have aged without your noticing. Remove things that could make you trip, broken bones are more likely and take longer to heal after 60. While you still have a steady income do large capital repairs and upgrades, even convert a room to a granny flat. This allows family to visit easier and if you need help there is a comfortable place for the helper to stay. The granny flat could also be a future source of income, for homestay students, tourists with Air BNB, and similar.

If your house is too big to cope with and the cleaning and maintenance is becoming too much for you, sell it just before you retire so you get used to your new location. Do this before you have to adjust to the random unstructured life of retirement! If you really hate gardening and mowing the lawn, sell the house and move to a unit with no garden upkeep on your part. If moving consider the distance to high quality health care and family. Do this a couple of years before you retire so you get to know the neighbours and settle in rather than waiting till after you retire and suddenly having no job and no familiar faces, it could prove traumatic.

Be realistic about what the costs will be. When planning for retirement income work out what you currently spend, you should spend less in retirement as you do not need business clothes and you are not travelling to work every day, you do not need to buy lunch out when you are at home. However you will still want entertainment, treats and holidays, even if for 6 days you do not work and have the 7th as a day of rest. Calculate the cost of such holidays and add 20 % for inflation, now you are ready to work out how much you will have need of in your savings.

Work out what you think you need for food, clothing, general expenses, accommodation, utilities, medical and transport and add 10%, just to be sure!

If you can work part time before you retire it will help you adjust to the random unstructured life of retirement. You will find that people will assume you have nothing to do and you will have so many requests for help and company, clubs to join, and charities to help that you will need to learn to say, sorry I am unavailable.

Prepare yourself for life as a volunteer, which is both demanding and rewarding. When you help others you are actually helping yourself. The feel good factor is great. There are so many things to do. Meals on Wheels are always short, charity shops love volunteers, councils have volunteers escorting tourists, museums of all kind need volunteers, language classes need fluent speakers to help the learners, schools always need helpers, nursing homes love visitors, there are craft groups that make clothes for homeless and refugees, housebound need shoppers and others need transport. This is just the tip of the iceberg. There are also lots of classes to learn all the things that you never had time for when working.

Did I mention grandchildren? If you are blessed with grandchildren this is the time when you will have some serious fun! I have my own train set among other toys. The crafts and extensive library are also well used. I also learned to make balloon animals after retirement it was and is such a joy.

Follow your dreams to do all the things you have always wanted to do, such as traveling, learn to draw, or even write a book!

Retirement

- **Before you retire get your home set up to be low maintenance.**

- **Be realistic about what the costs will be.**

- **Work out what you think you need and add 20%, just to be sure.**

- **If you can work part time before you retire it will help you adjust to the random unstructured life of retirement.**

- **Prepare yourself for life as a volunteer, which is both demanding and rewarding.**

- **If you are blessed with grandchildren this is the time when you will have some serious fun.**

- **If your house is too big to cope with, sell it just before you retire so you get used to your** new location before you adjust to the random unstructured life of retirement.

- Follow your dreams to do all the things you have always wanted to do, such as traveling, learn to draw, or even write a book.

Chapter 15

WILLS

What is a will? Wills are documents in which people, known as testators, give instructions about what is to happen to their property when they die. The will normally specifies the people who are to carry out the terms of the will (the executors), and sometimes also gives instructions about funeral arrangements. People who die intestate (without a valid will) lose the opportunity to give directions about how their property (deceased estate) will be apportioned. This means that the government office of the Public Trustee, will decide who gets your Star Wars collection and other important things. They will charge fees for this, so nothing may be left to distribute to anyone.

A will is one of the most important documents that a person will sign during their lifetime. As soon as you have a job and an income you need a will. There are really simple will kits available from newsagents and post offices that you can complete yourself, for less than $30. Alternatively, you could use Google to find a template and advice for free to write your own will. The catch is there is a lot of advertising and suggestions that you might find complicated. If you feel you can't complete it correctly you should hire the services of a solicitor or the Public Trustee.

Note that the Public Trustee will either offer to write up your will for free, but then insist that they become the executor of your estate and charge for that service out of your deceased estate once you die. Otherwise, they can charge you a fee (the same way as a Lawyer) for creating your will, if you choose to assign another person to be the executor of your deceased estate. You can find the links to the Public Trustee in each state at the end of this book in the Useful Links Section.

If you are single and leave everything to your parents or siblings, you can easily change it later. You absolutely must have a will if you have bought a house, have superannuation, got married, had children or have others depending on you. Do not be morbid about it. Celebrate the things you have to share.

If you are in your teens, it may come as a shock that you are not bulletproof. More men die in car crashes between the ages of 17 to 19 than any other age group. If you have a car you need a will.

Get neighbours or friends, two of them, to witness your will. Make sure these witnesses are not mentioned in your Will, otherwise it will be invalid. (Many people may prefer that a Justice of the Peace be one of their witnesses, though the law does not require it.)

WILLS

If you are married, remember your partner also needs to write his or her own will. Once you have written your will, clearly label it in an envelope and tell those who need to know where it is. If you want to make it easier for those you leave behind here are some things you might want to include in that envelope:

- a copy of your birth certificate;
- birth certificates of your parents;
- your marriage certificate;
- any Decree Nisi (Certificate of Divorce), if you have been divorced;
- all your account numbers, including the bank and branch;
- your insurance policy details including policy numbers, insurance company name, type of cover, and their contact details.
- You should check that your will is still valid every few years and make sure the other details in the envelope are still correct.

Remember, it is not about you, it is helping those who have to do the paperwork at a tough time. These certificates will be needed for your death certificate.

Here is a list of frequently asked questions, which can be found on the Public Trustee's website:

www.publictrusteesaustralia.com/faqs

WILLS

Some Questions and Answers which may help:

Q: What happens if I die without leaving a Will?
A: Your assets will be distributed according to a formula commonly referred to as the Laws of Intestacy, and not necessarily in accordance with your wishes.

Q: How old do I have to be to make a Will?
A: You are legally able to make a Will after you have attained 18 years of age.

Q: If I get married after I have made my Will, is that Will still valid?
A: No. Marriage revokes a Will, unless the Will has been made in contemplation of marriage.

Q: Will my spouse automatically receive my assets if I leave no Will?
A: No. The assets may also be shared with your children.

Q: If I divorce my spouse and die without updating my Will, will he or she receive any of my estate?
A: No. Divorce revokes any provision made under your Will for your ex-spouse.

Q: What if I die without a Will and I'm living in a de facto relationship?
A: A de facto partner of two years or more may be entitled to share in your estate

Q: Is a hand written Will valid?
A: Yes, if made in compliance with the Wills Act 1968.

WILLS

Q: If I die without a Will and have no family, who gets my assets?
A: If you leave no spouse or children and have no next of kin extending as far as cousins or their children, the ACT Government is entitled to the estate.

Q: What happens if the person who witnesses my Will is a beneficiary?
A: That beneficiary may be excluded from benefiting under your Will.

Q: Who may witness my Will?
A: Witnessing provision varies from State/Territory however generally any two persons together at the same time who are not beneficiaries or related to beneficiaries are valid witnesses for your Will. One pen should be used to avoid questions of validity.

If your will is deemed to be invalid the Public Trustee gets to sort out who gets what, if there is anything left after they have deducted their fees. When it comes to wills, also known as a person's Last Testament, there are some important points to follow to make sure that the will's authenticity is not questioned. Some of the main points are listed below.

The Will must be signed by each person using the same pen (preferably blue, but black is also accepted).

You should not pin or staple a will together nor to any other piece of paper.

Each and every page must be signed by the testator and both witnesses (signed not just initialed).

There must be two witnesses present, at the same time, when the testator signs his/her will.

The testator must have the mental capacity to understand what he or she has written and signed.

Neither the testator nor any witness may be intoxicated, or under the influence of drugs (or medications that affect alertness) at time of signing.

No witness must be a beneficiary or executor for the estate specified in the will.

You should create a new will whenever you have a new child, get married, divorced, or a child or spouse or other specified beneficiary in your will dies. Most people don't realise that any of these events can make your existing will invalid, and the government gets to decide how your deceased estate is distributed.

Wills

- **everyone over 18 needs one**

- **witnesses cannot be beneficiaries**

- **simple wills can use do it yourself forms,**

WILLS

complex need a solicitor

- **all witnesses should use the same biro preferably blue abut black will do**
- **make it easy for those left behind with extra documents**
- tell everyone where it is.

Chapter 16

E.P.A. & G.P.A.

When it come to your finances, there is a very powerful document, which most people are not even aware exists! An **Enduring Power of Attorney - E.P.A.** (not to be confused with a General Power of Attorney document).

Each person should have such a document once they are 18 years or older. This document comes into effect as soon as you become incapacitated in an accident, and for the duration of your incapacitation. This document gives the person you appoint the power to decide what hospital treatments you undergo, and gives them the ability to access your finances to pay your bills, and anything else you specify, so that there is minimal disruption to your life once you are out of hospital again and can attend to your own affairs. Of course the document allows you to specify and limit what powers you give to someone in those situations. The person you specify is required to act according to the document, and if they fail to do so they can be held liable.

Scenario:

Let's take a recent example of a 23 year old who has been working very hard and saved up enough money to go overseas on a holiday to Bali, and he doesn't have an EPA. He goes diving while swimming and lands on his head and becomes a quadriplegic. They treat him in the local hospital and then fly him home to Australia. Now he can't sign his name to access the funds in his bank account, so he can't pay his phone or internet bills, he can't pay his credit cards, and he can't pay his mortgage. He may want to get a special wheelchair but he can't deal with his health insurance company because he is incapacitated. He can't get his parents or girlfriend to do anything on his behalf, or apply for him to get Centrelink benefit payments either, simply because the government, banks, insurance companies, telcos, utilities such as electricity, water, and council rates will not recognise anyone as having power to act on his behalf. Then his parents may have to apply to the courts to grant them such powers, but this could take more than two years. In the meantime, his credit rating is ruined, and his life and the life of his parents and girlfriend are a nightmare.

You may say, I'm not going overseas, so I don't need one. Well, I ask you, what would be different if you were hit by a car walking across the street, or slipped in the shower at home and knocked yourself unconscious and were placed in a temporary coma, or you had a botched up medical operation leaving you incapacitated? It is no different. Such a document would allow the person or persons you nominate to attend to your financial affairs while you are in hospital, or decide what medical treatments you undergo in the event that you have been brought in to a hospital in an unconscious state.

There are two occasions that an E.P.A. loses its power: (a) when you are able to manage to your own financial affairs or communicate your wishes to the doctors in a hospital, and (b) in the event that you die, at which point a will (also known as a Last Testament) will take over. If you have trouble filling out an E.P.A. you can ask the Public Trustee to write one up for you, otherwise all you need to do is get it witnessed at a Justice of the Peace. Each adult in your family should have an E.P.A. even if you are lucky enough to never have the situation arise where it needs to be used.

A Power of Attorney is the legal power to make decisions on someone else's behalf. A **General Power of Attorney** document (**G.P.A.**) loses its power if you become incapacitated, where an Enduring Power of Attorney document (E.P.A.) continues even if the person giving it loses the capacity to make decisions. G.P.As and E.P.As are only valid in Australia, and have no legal effect in other countries.

If you give someone a general power of attorney, for instance to sign documents for you in your absence, that power will immediately end if for some reason you lose your capacity to make decisions. This could be very awkward if your attorney is in the process of conducting business affairs for you. Therefore, giving someone enduring power means that he/she is able to continue to act for you if you lose capacity to act for yourself. You may give your attorney power to make decisions about: personal/health matters; financial matters.

Examples of personal/health matters are decisions about where and with whom you live, whether you work or undertake education or training, whether you apply for a licence or permit, day-to-day issues like diet and dress, and whether to consent, refuse to consent or withdraw consent to particular types of health care for you (such as an operation). Without an E.P.A., the doctor who is treating you in hospital has the power to make these decisions, not your parents, spouse, partner or girlfriend. This usually upsets your loved ones when they discover that they can't have your wishes followed.

An example of a financial matter is deciding how your income should be invested."

You can download the E.P.A short form (for one attorney to attend to both your financial and health matters):

http://www.publicguardian.qld.gov.au/__data/assets/pdf_file/0007/269413/Enduring-Power-of-Attorney-Short-Form_Form-2.pdf

https://www.qld.gov.au/law/legal...and.../power-of-attorney.../power-of-attorney

You can download the E.P.A long form (for an

attorney(s) to attend to your financial and a different attorney(s) to attend to your health matters) with variations for each state by simply doing a web search for Enduring power of attorney, all the various options are on the first and second screens, avoid the ad sites.

If at any time that you have capacity you decide to cancel your E.P.A. you can do so by completing a revocation of enduring power of attorney the following, form from the same sites. But if you just want to change your existing E.P.A. you can do so by just completing a new E.P.A.

If you wish to give someone Power of Attorney to handle your finances only while you have capacity, such as going interstate or overseas, or you just can't get out or a hospital bed because of a broken leg, but you still have full capacity, then you will need a General Power of Attorney form. It only remains in effect as long as you have capacity. You can download the G.P.A. form below. Any adult can witness this form. If you wish to give the attorney the ability to handle matters involving the transfer of land on your behalf you will need to get it witnessed in front of a Justice of the Peace:

https://publications.qld.gov.au/dataset/0e798d96-9ba6-4aa0-95cd-5a017a0589a9/resource/efdfcdd4-2cf2-4002-992b-ec3e2b24d4a7/download/generalpowerofattorneyform1.pdf

E.P.A.s & G.P.A.s

- Each adult should have an E.P.A.

- E.P.A. allows someone to make decisions about your health and medical treatments while you are incapacitated.

- E.P.A. allows someone to attend to your finances while you are incapacitated.

- G.P.A allows someone to attend to your finances while you have capacity.

- G.P.A and E.P.A are only valid in Australia, and have no legal effect overseas.

- E.P.A must be witnessed in front of a Justice of the Peace.

- G.P.A can be witnessed by any adult and only needs to be witnessed in front of a Justice of the Peace if property (land) transfers are involved.

Chapter 17

A.H.D.

When it come to your health there is a very powerful document for those who live in the state of Queensland, Australia. This document is even more specific than an Enduring Power of Attorney document when dealing with your health while incapacitated, and is usually used in conjunction with an Enduring Power of Attorney document.

The **Advance Health Directive (A.H.D.)** is a document that states your wishes or directions regarding your future health care for various medical conditions. It comes into effect only if you are unable to make your own decisions. You may wish your directive to apply at any time when you are unable to decide for yourself, or you may want it to apply only if you are terminally ill. You should think clearly about what you would want your medical treatment to achieve if you become ill.

For example:

- If treatment could prolong your life, what level of quality of life would be acceptable to you?
  - How important is it to you to be able to communicate with family and friends?

- How will you know what technology is available for use in certain conditions?
- It is strongly recommended that you discuss the A.H.D. form with your doctor before completing it. In addition, a doctor must complete Section 5 of the form.

The purpose of an Advance Health Directive is to give you confidence that your wishes regarding health care will be carried out if you cannot speak for yourself. However, a request for euthanasia would not be followed, as this would be in breach of the law. Under the Queensland Criminal Code, it is a criminal offence to accelerate the death of a person by an act or omission. It is also an offence to assist another person to commit suicide. Other states have similar rules.

You will need to be aware that an A.H.D. is only valid in the state that it is written, other states have their own forms in Australia. According to information from the Office of the Public Guardian, some other states in Australia may choose to follow the A.H.D., but they are not obliged to do so. Also a doctor in Queensland may choose to ignore certain sections of an A.H.D. only if it is deemed best practice to do so. You can contact the Office of the Public Guardian who can answer questions you might have about completing an A.H.D. Alternatively, the A.H.D. form contains most of the information you require, and can be downloaded by searching **advanced health care directive** then selecting the appropriate state.

A.H.D.

- It is only valid in the state it is written unless otherwise stated

- It is more powerful and specific than an E.P.A. when dealing with your health requests while incapacitated

- It is usually used together with an E.P.A.

- It requires your family doctor to complete the doctor's section, and must be witnessed in front of a Justice of the Peace.

Chapter 18

INSURANCE

When it comes to insurance there are many different types. There is home insurance, contents insurance, car insurance, landlord's protection insurance, mortgage default insurance, health insurance, travel insurance, life insurance, accident insurance, income protection insurance, pet insurance, and finally there is also funeral insurance. There is also one more type of 'insurance', although technically it's not insurance, but still sold by insurance companies, called an annuity.

Read the fine-print of your policy carefully. Most policies have a clause that states if you are an undischarged bankrupt then your insurance becomes void and they don't have to pay your claims. In addition, when it comes to home contents insurance, if anyone living in your house with you is an undischarged bankrupt or has been convicted of a criminal offence within the last 5 years, your insurance may also be voided. When it comes to car insurance if anyone driving your car is an undischarged bankrupt or has been

INSURANCE

convicted of a criminal offence within the last 5 years and they have an accident in your car then your insurance may also be void. Note that in Queensland drink driving is considered a criminal offence, so be careful who you let drive your car or live in your home.

We will examine each of these insurances in turn:

Home Insurance:

Insures your home against damage to the house itself. For example, storms, falling trees, fire, etc.

- It does not cover anything outside which is not part of your house, such as a garden or fence, except for pools and spas, if they have been specified.
- It does not cover things inside the house that can be removed, such as blinds, carpets, curtains, floor coverings, and all your personal belongings.
- It does cover items which are hard-wired to your home, such as wall oven, cooking top, air-conditioners, water heaters.
- Usually includes liability cover against accidents in the home or property. For example, a visitor or workman injures themselves when a stair railing comes loose, or they trip on your carpet, or a loose tile.
- Is mandatory if you have a mortgage on the

INSURANCE

house. Once it is yours it is just as important to have.

- If you cannot afford the insurance, shop around for a better deal, but make sure you have it.
- If your house is underinsured (for example by 50%, then if you have a damage claim of part of the house, the insurance company will only pay you 50% of what the cost of the repair is).

Contents Insurance:

Insures items within your home which are not part of the physical house itself. This includes all your furniture, gadgets, belongings, and anything else you decide to insure. It also includes such things as carpets, blinds and curtains, floor coverings (except for tiles - which are covered by home insurance), fridges, washing machines, dryers, microwaves, etc.

This type of insurance is important if you have lots of stuff, or if floor coverings, blinds and curtains are not included in house cover.

You really need to read the fine print on these policies. Some only give a current depreciated value for a loss, a 10 year old carpet may be valued at $50, yet will cost over $500 to replace. And some only allow new-for-old, which could mean you get vouchers to buy replacement items at a store chosen by the insurance company, or

INSURANCE

they send you replacement items that you may not have wanted to buy. Some locate the exact item and replace it at no cost to you. I like insurance policies that offer to give you an agreed cash amount paid into your bank account so you can buy whatever you like with the money. You may choose, for example, to replace your old desk top computer set up with a lap top in a different brand.

Car Insurance

There are four types of car insurance, compulsory third-party property insurance, third-party insurance, fire & theft insurance, comprehensive insurance.

Compulsory third-party property insurance (CTPP) is mandatory for all registered cars, and in Queensland it is paid as part of your car registration each year (although you can choose who you want your insurer to be). This insurance covers you if your car causes damage to a fence, a house, or a person that the car hits, regardless who is driving. It covers you for anything that is not on the road. In some states you may have to purchase this insurance separately. Remember it is against to law to have a car driving or even parked on a road or public carpark, if it is not registered or does not have CTPP insurance.

Third-party insurance (TPI) insures another car and its passengers when your car hits the other car, and you are deemed at fault. Your car is not insured and you will have to pay for your own car repairs yourself.

INSURANCE

Fire & Theft insurance (FT-TPI) insures another car and its passengers when your car hits it and you are deemed at fault, even though you will have to pay for your own car repairs. However, if your car is stolen or burns in a fire your car will be covered. If you have an old clunker, or are a new driver without a driving history and comprehensive insurance premiums are almost as much as your car cost, then you should get Fire & Theft insurance, which is almost the same price at just TPI insurance (unless you live in a high theft suburb), because it gives you that extra cover against theft and fire.

Comprehensive insurance (CI) covers everything that FT-TPI covers, with the addition of covering your vehicle in an accident that you cause, and also your passengers. You need to read the fine print carefully because some comprehensive policies only cover your car up to a maximum of $3,000 if the other car that hit your car was not insured or the driver was drunk or under the influence of drugs, and they were deemed to be at fault. Also you might want to pay the extra $55 or so a year to get windscreen cover should a rock end up hitting your windscreen or another window and crack it. The cost to replace a windscreen in a new car can cost up to $1,300 so make sure you get the extra windscreen cover. If your car is worth it or you can't afford to replace it, you might need to consider getting comprehensive insurance. Remember, if you lease a car or have a car loan you will be required to have comprehensive car insurance.

INSURANCE

Landlord's protection insurance

Landlord's protection is very important if you have a rental property. If the tenants vandalise or burn down your place, you can pay out its mortgage; it also covers unpaid rent in some circumstances. If you have a rental property it would be hard to justify not having this insurance, it is also relatively cheap if you use a property manager. With a mortgage on the property it may also be required by the lender.

Mortgage Protection Insurance (or Mortgage Default Insurance)

This is a policy you pay to insure your bank against your defaulting on your mortgage. If you default on your mortgage because you become injured or lose your job, etc. they pay your bank. Their insurer then sells your house quickly at auction with no reserve for whatever they can get that day. You then owe the insurance company for any shortfall from the sale of your house that they had to pay the bank.

Remember, if you don't have at least a 20% deposit when buying your home the bank will require you to take out this insurance before they give you a home loan. See the chapter on Buying and Owning a House

This is a very unpleasant insurance, you do not want it. Avoid it by saving more before you buy a house and only buying one you can really afford, not one like your parents have after 40 years saving.

Health Insurance

Private health insurance is important if you are likely to need major surgery and do not have a good hospital with short waiting list nearby.

At the time of writing, the Australian government is considering means testing health insurance. If it passes into law it will mean if your income is above a certain amount you will be charged a tax (possibly equivalent to the cost of private health insurance) for failing to have private healthcare cover. There is currently an extra Medicare levy if you are on a high income without private insurance, on very high wages it can be dearer than having private cover, and yet you do not get the cover. Do the maths.

There is an age loading excess, which means that for every year that you do not have private health cover after the age of 30 your premium increases by 2% for each year. So, if you decide to take out private health insurance at the age of 60, you will pay an additional 60% premium each year, up to a maximum of 70%. After 10 years of continual cover that age excess is removed. All you need to do to avoid this is take out the most basic hospital cover, if you don't have any medical issues:

http://www.privatehealth.gov.au/healthinsurance/incenti

INSURANCE

vessurcharges/lifetimehealthcover.htm

There are different levels of hospital and extras cover, and each insurance company has different benefit packages. Select the company and cover that best suits your needs, remember you can always switch later. Each year you should check if your plan meets your needs, as you may still be on an old cover and paying more than new customers on newer plans. Insurance companies are known for doing that by not informing existing customers of cheaper newer plans that offer the same cover.

If you do need surgery, make sure you contact your insurance company for their no-gap providers list. Each surgeon or hospital has different agreements with different insurance companies. Where one insurance company can cover your operation with a specific doctor for no out-of-pocket costs, another insurance company may not have that doctor on their list, so you would have to pay part of the cost yourself, but they may have other doctors and hospitals with no-gap.

Make sure you read the policy details carefully. For example, in some insurance policies, failed births are not covered under a policy that includes child birth. You would have to pay for the whole hospital stay and doctors yourself. Read the fine-print!

Extras cover is important for dental, optical, etc. (if you do not have a health care card). The amount of the rebate for extras varies between 0% to 80% depending

INSURANCE

on your policy. If you are fairly healthy and only go to the dentist once a year, it is still cheaper to pay for 2 fillings than it is to pay the extras premium to only receive a 40% discount on the fillings. Most dentists give a 15% discount to cash only customers with no insurance, so the benefit of having extras cover is even less. For some major dental there is a 12 month or 2 year wait to be covered. Do the maths, and you will realise that the cost of a crown is less than the cost of two years extras cover. You need to have multiple problems each year to benefit from extras cover. Remember insurance companies are here to make a profit. If you need regular physiotherapy, wear spectacles, have major dental issues and have high prescription costs it may well be worth the cover. Again do the maths for you. You and your family are unique, so only you can work out what you spend.

Travel Insurance

If you are traveling overseas to countries like the United States where any medical procedure is outrageously expensive you will need travel insurance. For example, by searching the web you can see that if you injured a finger and had to have surgery on it in the United States, it would set you back USD$60,000. That's just for a single finger, it is much more if you needed to stay in hospital or had some serious illness or food poisoning you could end up with a debt in excess of one million U.S. dollars within just a few days. They won't let you leave their country to return home until you have paid the bill.

INSURANCE

Even if you do have travel insurance, you still need to read the policy carefully. Earlier this year there was an Australian couple who had the best travel insurance money could buy, but the wife had a premature birth (4 months early) on a flight to Hawaii. The new born child had to be in intensive care in a hospital so the wife stayed with the child in hospital in Hawaii. They were shocked to receive a US$1.6 million hospital bill that their travel insurance would not pay because births were not covered in their policy.

Life Insurance

Life insurance covers you if you become a paraplegic or quadriplegic or die. In some cases it even covers suicides, but usually after an extended period of cover.

Life insurance is important if you have a mortgage and if you have a family. If you are the main family income earner and you die you want to make sure your family does not become homeless. Make certain the payout amount is enough to cover the amount of the mortgage plus 10%.

Many life insurance policies become more expensive each year, for example one premium that I checked for $100 000 death cover that had been in place and paid for the previous 40 years the premium for the year after turning 60 was $1000 per month. That means despite the previous 40 years of cover, the whole cost of the payout would be charged in premiums within the following 7 years. The premium at 70 was unbelievable.

INSURANCE

It is good while you are young and have a mortgage and school fees but it becomes less viable as you age. Read the small print and make sure, even if it is paid by automatic bank debit and especially if it is paid automatically, that you check that the premiums are fair and if it is the appropriate cover for you. Many superannuation policies have life insurance in them and at a cheaper rate than outside the superannuation system, check first.

Accident Insurance

This insurance gives you a payout if you broke a bone, lost your sight, lost your hearing, become a paraplegic or quadriplegic or die as a result of an accident. It is not expensive, currently premiums range from $9.95 to $24.95 per month, but its payouts are not that great either.

You might have someone, such as Ace Insurance Group, trying to sell you this type of insurance over the phone one day. Unless you're accident prone you probably won't benefit from it. These payouts wouldn't even cover your medical expenses. Your health insurance probably covers you for accidents anyway.

Income Protection Insurance

This covers you if you lose your job or are injured and unable to work for a time. It is usually set at 75% of your regular wage. Payments of claims are paid for up to

12 months, and in certain events until your retirement age. Read the conditions carefully, it may not cover all the ways that you are unexpectedly without work.

If you have any debts or dependents this is a must, if you do not already have it as part of your superannuation scheme. Income protection is already included in most government superannuation schemes. Check if your superannuation has it included. Check if you are covered for the right amount.

Income protection insurance premiums are tax deductible in Australia. You can either deduct the premiums from your taxable income, or have it as part of your superannuation fund.

Funeral Insurance

This is one of those schemes where insurance companies make a lot of money from people who don't do their maths. At the time you take out funeral insurance you agree on a payout amount and pay the premiums until you die. These premiums usually increase with your age. The problem is, so does inflation. So by the time you die the payout doesn't come close to covering your funeral expenses. Over all those years you could have ended up paying more than 10 times the payout amount in their premium payments.

So unless you are terminally ill and will die in two years or so (Note: most won't pay if you die within the first 12 months anyway, some cover for accidental death though

INSURANCE

in this time), you wouldn't benefit from funeral insurance. Either prepay a funeral or make sure there is enough in the bank to pay for it. You could even open a separate bank savings account (in your spouse's name) where you deposit $2 a week to accumulate as your funeral account.

Annuities

This is even worse than funeral insurance schemes. An annuity is a contractually executed, relatively low-risk investment product, where the financial institution or insurance company agrees to pay you a fixed monthly or annual income for a certain number of years, or until you die.

If you die, the financial institution or insurance company keeps the money. It becomes their money the moment the contract is signed.

If the financial institution or insurance company goes bankrupt, you get nothing and your money is gone, as happened in several cases during the Global Financial Crisis.

Here is the most important thing of all. It's called the time-value of money. Let's say the annuity guarantees you an income of 10% per year. If you invested $100,000 then you expect to get 10% each year. That sounds good at the start. But at that rate you might think it would take you 10 years to get back the money you invested. Wrong! You had to pay tax on the money they paid to you, so let's say you are in the 34% tax bracket, then it would take you 16.6 years to get back the money that you originally invested in an annuity. But it is worse than that, because had you left that money in a simple bank savings account at a conservative 3% p.a. interest rate, you missed out on another 55.7% interest over the 16.6 years (It's more likely that the interest rate would average 6.5% over that period, so you would have earned a lot more). On top of all that, the regular 10% payment each month loses its value with inflation each year and will probably buy you only 14% of what it did 16.6 years earlier.

Scenario 1:

Person invests $100,000 in an annuity at 10% p.a. Each month they receive a payment of $550 after tax (assuming 34% income tax). After 16.6 years they have received $100,000, which is what they originally invested.

Scenario 2:

Person leaves $100,000 in the bank earning just 3% p.a. interest with compounding interest after 16.6 years they earned $55,796 interest, plus they still have the original $100,000. So they have a total of $155,796 in their hands. With compounding interest this amount rapidly doubles in just a few more years, while the annuity in 'scenario 1' still keeps paying the same amount.

Why would anyone ever consider getting an annuity? All

INSURANCE

the financial institution does is put your money in a bank account like the person in Scenario 2 and they keep the difference instead of you.

Insurance Problems

If you can't solve problems with your insurance company you can contact the Financial Ombudsman Service (FOS) for assistance. The contact details for the FOS are:

>Mail: GPO Box 3, MELBOURNE VIC 3001
>Telephone: 1300 78 08 08
>Facsimile: (03) 9613 6399
>Website: www.fos.org.au
>E-mail: info@fos.org.au

Again, I repeat this advice is of a general nature and may not be appropriate for your circumstances, see disclaimer page.

Insurance

- **Check what you actually need**

- **Get what you actually need**

- **Read all of the fine print**

- **Know what it covers**

- **Contact Financial Ombudsman Service if you need help**

Chapter 19
TOYS

Toys are anything that is fun to have and fun to play with, but not essential. They are extras. For children, toys are an integral part of their learning. However, for adults it is a description of anything amusing that costs money, a thing that is not needed, but makes you feel happy.

Because they are considered as extras, always make sure you pay your mortgage first, then all your other essential costs. Mostly these toys give you a high that is similar to going for a walk in the park or picnic with a good friend. So why not go for that walk, connect with the environment and feel good instead of buying that toy. Do not waste what you do not have on things that are unnecessary, often clutter your house, and have ongoing costs like upgrades, batteries, extra games, matching shoes, etc. Well, you get the idea...

When it comes to cars, only get one if you really need one, like when there is no appropriate public transport. You might not realise, but those stretch Volvos (buses) can get you to where you need, if you live in the city or in a large country community. Trains are brilliant, if you are fortunate enough to have one nearby. Consider this: If you were visiting another city on holiday, you would probably use their local transport to explore, so why not have a holiday at home. Take a cruise on the ferries, visit suburbs and take advantage of the free open days at various places of interest. How about expanding your mind at a museum or art gallery. Most are close to busses and trains. Dare I say it? Try walking, that way you don't need to spend money at a gym.

When it comes to shiny things, keep them to a minimum. Always pay in cash after you have saved up for it and negotiated for the best price. Most shiny things become out of date very quickly, so you will need to buy more to upgrade or replace them. So, if you do not need it, do not buy it. It's that simple! See the chapter on buying things.

Toys

- **Pay your mortgage first, then if you have anything left put it into your mortgage to get rid of it fast.**

- **Cars, only if you really need one and there is no appropriate public transport.**

- **Shiny things, keep them to a minimum and pay cash after you have saved and negotiated for the best deal.**

TOYS

- **Re-read the chapter on buying things.**

Chapter 20

CHILDREN

Toys are an integral part of children's learning. The most popular toys are cardboard boxes. They are the most versatile and keep your children occupied the longest. Books and cuddly toys are next, followed by building blocks and bicycles. Cardboard boxes can be obtained for free from supermarkets in various sizes to become cubby houses, trains, rockets...You name it, their imagination will take them there. While cuddly toys are nice, children really only need one for comfort and another one to play with. Your friends and parents will most likely supply them when they find out a child is about to join your family. The same applies for building blocks and bicycles. As a parent your job is to love them, teach them right from wrong, educate your children, feed them and clothe them.

Children do not need to have the latest promotional items seen on television or in the movies. They have never needed those items and never will. Your children will probably spend more time playing with the boxes those items came in. However, you can find some amazing toys at charity shops, often donated by people whose children never played with them, because they were too busy watching TV or playing on a computer. They are a great spot to find jigsaw puzzles, but make sure all the pieces are still in the box.

Their shoes need to fit, not have name brands. When your children are growing rapidly and their shoe size seems to be changing every month they will only need two pairs of shoes. The one pair for school and going out, and the other for getting really grubby when playing. Again, grandparents really love buying really cute shoes with sparkles and flashing lights. Let them; just make sure they know the correct size for when they feel the need to shop.

Spend time with your children. You can never get that time back once they have grown up and you were too busy or too stressed. Go to the park, play cricket in the back yard, visit museums or laugh in the art galleries. You will all be glad that you did. All these things are free. If they are watching TV watch it with them and discuss what's on. Often children misinterpret and get very upset from something quite harmless. Your presence will make them feel safe and you also get to know what they are watching.

Read to them. By reading to children you are aiding in their development, sparking their imaginations and teaching them the value of the written word. You will also have fun enjoying the stories yourself. Read fact and fiction to them. As they reach the age of seven you

CHILDREN

should stop at the thrilling parts and say you will read them the next chapter tomorrow, unless they want to read the chapter to you now to find out what happens next. Always enjoy the time with your children.

Play with them. I learned to love playing trains and now have my own wooden train set that I play with when my grandchildren visit. We build amazing towers, train bridges, some are even on wheels. It even pleases their parents that we are having so much fun. Babysitting isn't a chore, it's FUN! We also have a kite that we fly in a nearby park, which we walk to. Life is good.

Love your children. Teach them to love and respect others. Until you respect yourself you cannot respect others. Self-respect is worth having. Teach them it's alright and appropriate to say 'I don't like that'. Help them find what they are good at and let them do it. When they try but fail, make sure you are there to catch them, remind them that you still love them. Next time, they just might succeed. Love them unconditionally.

Teach them the value of money by teaching them how to allocate their pocket money. Ideally they should allocate 1/3 to spend on the things they want, 1/3 to save for special things, and 1/3 to share with others. If they are saving up for something, do not give them half the money so that they can have it earlier. Do not give them too much; otherwise there is no incentive for them to get a part time job when they are in their teens. This teaches them responsibility, pride in their work, and good money management.

CHILDREN

As a family consider sponsoring an overseas child. Follow what is happening to the child, their education and lifestyle. This will help your children understand just how much that they do have compared to other children in the world. It also helps them learn geography. It's also one of the first stages of philanthropy, as is buying a toy to put under a community Christmas tree for underprivileged children. My children used to love selecting toys with care, then wrapping them up to put under a community Christmas tree. Now that they are all grown up, with children of their own, they are still loving and generous men.

Get a pet to teach your children responsibility and care. Teach them how to look after the pet and to love it. Don't worry; the pet will remind your children if they forget to feed it. If an appropriate pet is chosen, it will also love your children back. Aggressive animals or a 'nice' animal from an aggressive breed is never appropriate, unless you want the mock sympathy from front page on the tabloids when your child is attacked and scarred for life. Or even worse... killed! You are ultimately responsible for the choice of pet. Do not choose a big or muscly watch-dog because you think it will make you look stronger. It won't do that, but it may end up emotionally scaring your whole family and your neighbours. Never, ever, leave a child under the age of 13 alone with a dog for any reason.

At a small age assign your children appropriate jobs to contribute and maintain the house. A two-year-old child

CHILDREN

can pull a quilt over a bed and pick up their own toys and place them into an easy access toy box. A child aged three can put washing into the laundry basket. A five-year-old can make a bed. While, a seven -year-old can vacuum a bedroom, and put their own clean washing into their drawers. A child aged 12 can do their own washing and ironing and clean a bathroom or a toilet. Have set tasks each week for everyone in your household to do. If both parents are working sit down with the whole family to select tasks. For example, cleaning the bathroom takes longer but is less yucky than cleaning the toilet, so those tasks can be considered equivalent. Vacuuming the lounge is quicker and less messy than scrubbing the kitchen floor, so those tasks can be also be considered equivalent. No one gets paid for performing these. If you live in the house, eat the food and make the clothes dirty, you should be helping with the work involved. You can make sure that pocket money is withheld if the tasks are not done, and their friends will only be allowed to visit when they have tidied up their rooms. This teaches them respect for friends and action-consequence.

Start a small education account with small automatic contributions from your main bank account. This fund will be used to pay for their education expenses, excursions, textbooks, uniforms, computers, etc. Education accounts are treated differently for taxes and charges, so check out the latest tax rules and shop around for the best account. If you decide that you want your children to attend a private school you will need to make those automatic contributions large ones. Check out the various private school fees and ask them how much extras will realistically amount to. Work out a timescale and the actual charges for such things as music lessons or coaching. Then do the maths. You had better start saving long before your child has their first birthday!

Children

- Children do not need to have the latest promotional items shown on television. They never have, and they never will.

- Their shoes need to fit, not have name brands.

- Spend time with them.

- Read to them.

- Play with them.

- Love them and teach them to love and respect others.

- Teach them the value of money.

- As a family sponsor an overseas child.

- Get a pet to teach them responsibility and care.

CHILDREN

- **At young age give them appropriate jobs to contribute and maintain the house to earn pocket money. Don't just give them pocket money for doing nothing.**

- **Start a small education account with small automatic contributions from your bank account.**

- **If you want your children to go to private schools make sure those automatic contributions large ones. You better start saving long before their first birthday.**

Chapter 21

THE BUDGET

Ways to use this budget template:

- Follow it for a month or two just filling-in items as they occur.

- Help you plan for what you should be aiming for.

- Check how you well you are sticking to your budget.

- Changing your budget and plans as your income changes.

Ideally if you have two wages you should aim to live on just the one wage and put 80% of the smaller wage into your home loan while saving the other 20% for investments and holidays. The mortgage will disappear very quickly as there will be less interest to pay. Depending on your home loan interest rate this can end up saving you more than 15 years of interest on your home loan. It's simple. If you attack the principal by making these extra repayments, then there is less to

THE BUDGET

accrue in interest. The bonus is, if you budget on only having the one wage, when unemployment or maternity leave arises, you can carry on as normal. This is worth considering.

Actual Spending Type	Actual Amount	Frequency (d/w/m/y)	Weekly Total	Annual Total
House				
Rent / mortgage repayments	$	d | w | m | y	$	$
Repairs	$	d | w | m | y	$	$
Rates	$	d | w | m | y	$	$
Water	$	d | w | m | y	$	$
Electricity	$	d | w | m | y	$	$
Pool & garden	$	d | w | m | y	$	$
Food				
Groceries	$	d | w | m | y	$	$
Fruit & Veg	$	d | w | m | y	$	$
Bread/milk/eggs	$	d | w | m | y	$	$
Communications				
Phone	$	d | w | m | y	$	$
Internet	$	d | w | m | y	$	$
Mobiles	$	d | w | m | y	$	$
Computer	$	d | w | m | y	$	$
Printer ink/ paper	$	d | w | m | y	$	$
Insurance				
House & contents	$	d | w | m | y	$	$
Car	$	d | w | m | y	$	$
Life	$	d | w | m | y	$	$
Disability	$	d | w | m | y	$	$
Health	$	d | w | m | y	$	$
Medical				
Dentist	$	d | w | m | y	$	$
Optical	$	d | w | m | y	$	$
Doctor	$	d | w | m | y	$	$
Pharmacy	$	d | w | m | y	$	$
Alternate	$	d | w | m | y	$	$
Gym	$	d | w | m | y	$	$
Transport				
Fares	$	d | w | m | y	$	$
Car payments	$	d | w | m | y	$	$

THE BUDGET

Maintenance	$	d | w | m | y	$	$
Bike	$	d | w | m | y	$	$
Petrol	$	d | w | m | y	$	$
Clothing				
Needed	$	d | w | m | y	$	$
Wanted	$	d | w | m | y	$	$
Entertainment				
Going out	$	d | w | m | y	$	$
Eating out	$	d | w | m | y	$	$
Gambling	$	d | w | m | y	$	$
Alcohol/smokes/etc.	$	d | w | m | y	$	$
Sports	$	d | w | m | y	$	$
Magazines /newspapers	$	d | w | m | y	$	$
Parties	$	d | w | m | y	$	$
New games	$	d | w | m | y	$	$
Children's toys	$	d | w | m | y	$	$
Presents	$	d | w | m | y	$	$
Holidays	$	d | w | m | y	$	$
Donations				
Sponsorships	$	d | w | m | y	$	$
Direct donation	$	d | w | m | y	$	$
Education				
Fees	$	d | w | m | y	$	$
Books etc.	$	d | w | m | y	$	$
Excursions	$	d | w | m | y	$	$
Uniforms	$	d | w | m | y	$	$
Pets				
Food	$	d | w | m | y	$	$
Fleas & worms	$	d | w | m | y	$	$
Veterinary	$	d | w | m | y	$	$
Special savings				
Home	$	d | w | m | y	$	$
Car	$	d | w | m | y	$	$
Holiday	$	d | w | m | y	$	$

Chapter 22

EPILOGUE

Keep this book and read it again in six months to see if it has made a difference to your life and finances. Have you followed it? If you did and it helped you, I am glad. Tell your friends about this book and what you have learned. If this book didn't help you go and seek the help of a financial counsellor. Centrelink, Mission Australia, Lifeline, St. Vincent de Paul Society or the Salvation Army all have financial counsellors here to help. They will help you.

I believe that the following quotation concisely summarises what is needed for a healthy society. It also demonstrates wisdom, how to be healthy, wealthy and wise.

"Ephesians 4:25-29, 30-32a Good News Translation (GNT) [25]No more lying, then! Each of you must tell the truth to the other believer, because we are all members together in the body of Christ. [26]If you become angry, do not let your anger lead you into sin, and do not stay angry all day. [27]Don't give the Devil a chance. [28]If you used to rob, you must stop robbing and start working, in order to earn an honest living for yourself and to be able to help the poor. ^{29}Do not use harmful words, but only helpful words, the kind that build up and provide what is needed, so that what you say will do good to those who hear you. ^{31}Get rid of all bitterness, passion, and anger. No more shouting or insults, no more hateful feelings of any sort. ^{32}Instead, be kind and tender-hearted to one another, and forgive one another."

From the Good News Translation (GNT)
Copyright © 1992 by American Bible Society

Chapter 23

Useful Links

SELF-HELP LINKS

Quit smoking:
Quitline 13 78 48   www.quitnow.gov.au

Diet and health advice:
Diabetes Australia 1300 136 588
www.diabetesaustralia.com.au

Those with drinking problems:
Alcoholics Anonymous 1300 222 222
www.aa.org.au

Families of those with drinking problems:
Al-Anon 1300 252 666
www.al-anon.org/australia

Gambling problems:
Gamblers Anonymous (02) 9726 6625
www.gansw.org.au

Crisis support & suicide prevention:
Lifeline 13 11 14
www.lifeline.org.au

USEFUL LINKS

FINANCIAL LINKS

Compare Australian bank accounts:
Infochoice www.infochoice.com.au/banking

Compare payday loans:
Finder www.finder.com.au/payday-loans/compare

Compare credit cards:
www.creditcardfinder.com.au
www.creditcard4u.com.au
www.creditcards.com.au/compare

CHECK LICENCES LINKS

Tradesmen (builders, tilers, plumbers, electricians, etc.):
www.licensedtrades.com.au

Certified Practicising Accountants:
www.cpaaustralia.com.au/about-us/find-a-cpa

Chartered Accountants:
www.charteredaccountants.com.au/Chartered-Accountants/Find-a-Chartered-Accountant/Search-for-a-Chartered-Accountant

Certified Financial Planners:
www.fpa.asn.au

USEFUL LINKS

Queensland Licence search:
(Property agents, auctioneers, motor dealers, etc.)
www.qld.gov.au/law/laws-regulated-industries-and-accountability/queensland-laws-and-regulations/check-a-licence-association-charity-or-register/check-a-licence /

Business registration details:
www.abr.business.gov.au

Australian Securities & investments Commission (ASIC): www.asic.gov.au

Check vehicle registration (Queensland):
www.service.transport.qld.gov.au/checkrego/application/TermAndConditions.xhtml?windowId=915

DISPUTES & OMBUDSMAN LINKS

Australian consumer disputes:
www.consumerlaw.gov.au

Commonwealth Ombudsman: 1300 362 072
www.ombudsman.gov.au/pages/making-a-complaint/complaints-the-ombudsman-can-investigate/

- *Australian Government agencies and services disputes*
- *Australian Federal Police disputes*
- *Australian Defense Force disputes*
- *Freedom of Information disputes*
- *Immigration disputes*

USEFUL LINKS

- *Postal industry disputes*
- *Overseas students disputes*

Telecommunication Industry Ombudsman: 1800 062 058
www.tio.com.au/about-us

- *Telephone & mobile service provider disputes*
- *Internet service provider disputes*

Credit & Investments Ombudsman: 1800 138 422
www.cio.org.au
Financial services providers' disputes including:

- *lenders*
- *investment and financial planning services*
- *insurance*
- *non-bank lenders*
- *micro lenders*
- *finance brokers*
- *mortgage brokers*
- *lenders mortgage insurance*
- *accountants*
- *tax agents*
- *superannuation providers*
- *credit providers*
- credit unions and building societies

USEFUL LINKS

Financial Ombudsman Service: 1800 367 287
www.fos.org.au
Financial services providers' disputes including:
- *banks*
- *credit unions and building societies*
- *credit providers*
- *non-bank lenders*
- *finance brokers*
- *micro lenders*
- *investment and financial planning services*
- *insurance*
- *some superannuation providers*

Superannuation Complaints Tribunal: 1300 884 114
www.sct.gov.au
- *superannuation fund disputes*
- *annuities and deferred annuities disputes*
- *Retirement Savings Accounts disputes*

Private Health Insurance Ombudsman: 1800 640 695
www.phio.org.au
- private health insurance disputes

Produce and Grocery Industry Ombudsman: 1800 206 385
www.produceandgroceryombudsman.com.au
- *supply disputes of produce and groceries to markets*

USEFUL LINKS

and retailers

Public Transport Ombudsman (Victoria): 1800 466 865
www.ptovic.com.au
- *public transport disputes in Victoria*

Tolling Customer Ombudsman: 1800 145 000
www.tollingombudsman.com.au

Toll operator disputes including:
- *Airportlink M7*
- *CityLink*
- *EastLink*
- *Go Via*
- *Hills M2*
- *Roam and Roam Express*

Office of the Australian Information Commissioner: 1300 363 992
www.oaic.gov.au
- breach of privacy disputes

Australian Human Rights Commission: 1300 656 419
www.humanrights.gov.au
- *complaints about discrimination because of race, sex or disability*

Fair Work Ombudsman: 13 13 94
www.fairwork.gov.au

USEFUL LINKS

- *information and advice about your workplace rights and obligations*

PUBLIC TRUSTEE LINKS
www.publictrusteesaustralia.com/links

(NSW) Trustee & Guardian: 1300 364 103
www.tag.nsw.gov.au/enquiries-virtual.html

(VIC) State Trustees: 1300 138 672
www.statetrustees.com.au/contact-us /

(QLD) Public Trustee of Queensland: 1300 360 044
www.pt.qld.gov.au/contact/index.html

(WA) Public Trustee for Western Australia: 1300 746 116
www.publictrustee.wa.gov.au/_apps/contacts/

(SA) Public Trustee for South Australia: 1800 673 119
www.publictrustee.sa.gov.au/contact-us/

(TAS) Public Trustee for Tasmania:
Hobart (03) 6235 5200
Launceston (03) 6335 3400
Burnie (03) 6430 3600
Devonport (03) 6430 3690
www.publictrustee.tas.gov.au/contact/

(ACT) Public Trustee for the ACT: (02) 6207 9800
www.publictrustee.act.gov.au/contact

USEFUL LINKS

(NT) The Public Trustee for the Northern Territory:
Darwin (08) 8999 7271
Alice Springs (08) 8952 5493
www.nt.gov.au/justice/pubtrust/index.shtml

RENTAL PROPERTY LINKS

QLD) Rights and obligations of landlords:
www.rta.qld.gov.au/~/media/Publications/Publications%20for%20managers/RTA_Managing%20general%20tenancies%20in%20Queensland.ashx

QLD) Rights and obligations of tenants:
www.rta.qld.gov.au/~/media/Forms/Forms%20for%20general%20tenancies/RTA-pocket-guide-for-tenants-house-and-units-form-17a.ashx

(NSW) Rights and obligations of landlords:
www.fairtrading.nsw.gov.au/ftw/Tenants_and_home_owners/Being_a_landlord.page

(NSW) Rights and obligations of tenants:
http://tenants.org.au/tenants-rights-factsheets

(VIC) Rights and obligations of landlords:
www.consumer.vic.gov.au/housing-and-accommodation/renting

(VIC) Rights and obligations of tenants:
www.consumer.vic.gov.au/library/Publications/Housing-and-accommodation/Renting/Renting-a-home-a-guide-

USEFUL LINKS

for-tenants.pdf

(TAS) Rights and obligations of landlords and tenants:
www.consumer.tas.gov.au/renting

(SA) Rights and obligations of landlords and tenants:
www.sa.gov.au/__data/assets/pdf_file/0012/12072/Information_brochure.pdf

(WA) Rights and obligations of landlords and tenants:
www.commerce.wa.gov.au/consumer-protection/renting-home

NEIGHBOURHOOD DISPUTE RESOLUTION LINKS

Disputes about fences, trees and buildings:
www.qld.gov.au/law/housing-and-neighbours/disputes-about-fences-trees-and-buildings

Neighbourhood Mediation Kit:
https://publications.qld.gov.au/dataset/17cb1543-c4af-495d-9412-f43f673dc79e/resource/050c6991-1e22-4933-b185-c92f770eb78a/download/neighbourhoodmediationkit.pdf

USEFUL LINKS

WEDDINGS & MARRIAGE LINKS

Getting married information:
www.qld.gov.au/law/births-deaths-marriages-and-divorces/marriage-weddings-and-registered-relationships/getting-married/

Find a Marriage Celebrant:
www.celebrations.org.au/ceremonies/134-fast-find-a-celebrant/1652-regions

(QLD) Form to register a relationship - both partners:
https://publications.qld.gov.au/dataset/8f1d4035-229e-4870-822e-baa63a59eb8b/resource/c6947b49-3c4d-4698-80cb-f6dda18abaf6/download/registeracivilpartnershipsubmission.pdf

(QLD) Form to terminate a relationship - both partners:
https://publications.qld.gov.au/storage/f/2014-04-17T00%3A55%3A49.736Z/application-to-terminate-a-registered-relationship-form-18.pdf

(QLD) Statutory declaration to terminate a relationship - either partner can apply without the other present.
https://publications.qld.gov.au/storage/f/2014-04-17T00%3A58%3A24.768Z/registered-relationship-termination-statutory-declaration.pdf

USEFUL LINKS

DIVORCE LINKS

Divorce Fact Sheet:
http://www.familycourt.gov.au/wps/wcm/connect/36763cca-8b01-4f40-9e7e-f8e2e590189f/Preparing_affidavit0313V2.pdf?MOD=AJPERES&CONVERT_TO=url&CACHEID=36763cca-8b01-4f40-9e7e-f8e2e590189f

Application for divorce kit:
http://www.familycourt.gov.au/wps/wcm/connect/d9c6e4be-3288-4fc5-9080-e0ffb759beee/Divorce_Kit_0313_V3a.pdf?MOD=AJPERES&CONVERT_TO=url&CACHEID=d9c6e4be-3288-4fc5-9080-e0ffb759beee

Divorce service kit:
http://www.familycourt.gov.au/wps/wcm/connect/6bca8754-d4e7-4147-8929-7432f59e3d75/Divorce_ServiceKit_0313_V2b.pdf?MOD=AJPERES&CONVERT_TO=url&CACHEID=6bca8754-d4e7-4147-8929-7432f59e3d75

USEFUL LINKS

POWER OF ATTORNEY LINK

E.P.A short form (same attorney for health and finance):
https://publications.qld.gov.au/dataset/0e798d96-9ba6-4aa0-95cd-5a017a0589a9/resource/94c27605-28ad-4e71-846b-04b0d66ef3b8/download/enduringpowerofattorneyshortformform2.pdf

E.P.A long form (different attorney for health and finance):
https://publications.qld.gov.au/dataset/0e798d96-9ba6-4aa0-95cd-5a017a0589a9/resource/d33b1e89-0b07-4a14-a4d8-05ff4f610b25/download/enduringpowerofattorneylongformform3.pdf

Revocation of E.P.A. form:
https://publications.qld.gov.au/dataset/0e798d96-9ba6-4aa0-95cd-5a017a0589a9/resource/f94f016c-5fff-4b27-9f77-a957bd120865/download/revocationofenduringpowerofattorneyform6.pdf

G.P.A. form:
https://publications.qld.gov.au/dataset/0e798d96-9ba6-4aa0-95cd-5a017a0589a9/resource/efdfcdd4-2cf2-4002-992b-

USEFUL LINKS

ec3e2b24d4a7/download/generalpowerofattorneyform1.pdf

Revocation of G.P.A.
https://publications.qld.gov.au/dataset/0e798d96-9ba6-4aa0-95cd-5a017a0589a9/resource/8fed429e-c45b-4354-b079-21a7ed773174/download/revocationofgeneralpowerofattorneyform5.pdf

Advanced Health Directive (QLD) A.H.D. form:
https://publications.qld.gov.au/dataset/0e798d96-9ba6-4aa0-95cd-5a017a0589a9/resource/6a3af073-cdba-4b82-8de7-eabe65950c24/download/advancehealthdirectiveformform4.pdf

DEBT COLLECTOR & INSOLVENCY LINKS

Australian Financial Security Authority: 1300 364 785
www.afsa.gov.au

Your rights when approached by debt collectors:
www.accc.gov.au/consumers/debt-debt-collection/dealing-with-debt-collectors

In financial trouble information guide:
www.afsa.gov.au/debtors/in-financial-trouble

USEFUL LINKS

Personal insolvency information booklet:
www.afsa.gov.au/debtors/personal-insolvency-information-booklet/personal-insolvency-information-for-debtors

Forms for declaring an intention to present a debtor's petition:
www.afsa.gov.au/resources/forms/forms-for-declaring-an-intention-to-present-a-debtors-petition

Forms for declaring bankruptcy:
www.afsa.gov.au/resources/forms/forms-for-declaring-bankruptcy

Forms for bankruptcy by sequestration order:
www.afsa.gov.au/resources/forms/forms-for-bankruptcy-by-sequestration-order

Proposing a debt agreement:
www.afsa.gov.au/resources/forms/prescribed-information-1

Forms for proposing a personal insolvency agreement:
www.afsa.gov.au/resources/forms/forms-for-proposing-a-personal-insolvency-agreement

Form for a deceased person's insolvent estate:
www.afsa.gov.au/resources/forms/form-4-statement-of-affairs-under-part-xi-1

USEFUL LINKS

TELEPHONE & INTERNET LINKS

Voice over internet protocol (VoIP) providers list:
www.voipchoice.com.au

Internet service providers (ISP) list:
www.idd.com.au/internet-service-providers.php

Mobile carriers list:
www.idd.com.au/mobile-providers.php

Residential telephone providers list:
www.idd.com.au/telephone-companies.php

Virtual Private Network (VPN):

• Apple iPhones:
http://itunes.apple.com/us/app/openvpn-connect/id590379981?mt=8

• Android Mobiles:
http://play.google.com/store/apps/details?id=de.blinkt.openvpn

USEFUL LINKS

PRIVATE HEALTH INSURANCE LINKS

List of private health funds:
www.privatehealth.gov.au/dynamic/

Compare private health funds:
www.compareinsurance.com.au/health-insurance/insurers

No-gap cover lists:
www.privatehealth.gov.au/dynamic/gapdoctors.aspx

USEFUL LINKS

INSURANCE LINKS

Compare Home & Contents insurers:
www.compareinsurance.com.au/home-insurance/insurers

Compare Car insurers:
www.compareinsurance.com.au/car-insurance/insurers

Compare Travel insurers:
www.compareinsurance.com.au/travel-insurance/insurers

Compare Income Protection insurers:
www.compareinsurance.com.au/income-protection/insurers

Compare Motorbike insurers:
www.compareinsurance.com.au/motorbike-insurance/insurers

Compare Bicycle insurers:
www.compareinsurance.com.au/bike-insurance/insurers

Compare Pet insurers:
www.compareinsurance.com.au/pet-insurance/insurers

Compare Caravan & Mobile Home insurers:
www.compareinsurance.com.au/caravan-insurance/insurers

Travel Insurance information sheet:
http://smartraveller.gov.au/guide/all-travellers/insurance/

USEFUL LINKS

ABOUT THE AUTHOR

W. J. Scott (Dip.T., QUT, B.Ed UNE, Dip. F.S., F.P, Deakin, A.Dip F.S, F.P Deakin, M.TEFL, Teflink)

W.J. Scott started working at age 16. Later, having completed a Dip T in science became a high school teacher. After a few years teaching she also acquired a B.Ed. in counselling and Religious Education. During the 20 years or more as a teacher, students would often ask during Maths lessons for financial tips. After having spent most of a diverse career as a teacher trying to assist students become the best that they could be W.J. Scott saw the need to further study a Diploma and Advanced diploma in financial planning, and included some practical experience with financial planning.

This book was written at the request of people that were helped, so that they could have a reminder of where all the information that they needed was.

AVAILABLE BOOKS BY W.J.SCOTT

2015   The Perfect Assignment

2016   Debt Free: The Morals of Money Management

2016   Libre de Deuda: de la Moral de la Administración del Dinero

2016   Swift Simple Sweet...........

Available from:

Amazon Bookstore for Kindle versions
Apple iBookstore for iBooks versions

Contact the publisher for other versions

info@FelixPublishing.com

Contact the author
wjscott@FelixPublishing.com

I would love to hear from you, thank you for buying this book.

www.ingramcontent.com/pod-product-compliance
Lightning Source LLC
Chambersburg PA
CBHW070607300426
44113CB00010B/1435